CW01335777

FLYING SO HIGH

WEST HAM'S
CUP FINALS

Pete May

© Pete May 2012 all rights reserved

Pete May has asserted his rights under the
Copyright, Design and Patents Act, 1988, to be
identified as the author of this work. First published
in 2012 by Endeavour Press Ltd as an e-book and in
2015 as a paperback.

CONTENTS

1. SOME PEOPLE ARE ON THE PITCH...

1923 FA CUP FINAL

BOLTON WANDERERS 2 WEST HAM UNITED 0

Wembley Stadium, Saturday April 28 1923. Kick-off 3pm.

WEST HAM: Ted Hufton, Billy Henderson, Jack Young, Syd Bishop, George Kay, Jack Tresadern, Dick Richards, Billy Brown, Vic Watson, Billy Moore, Jimmy Ruffell.

IF THE KITS ARE UNITED: Claret and blue shirts with a lace-up round collar, baggy white shorts, claret socks and huge boots.

FACIAL HAIR: Gaffer Syd King and trainer Charlie Paynter sport bank manager's moustaches, but the rest of the side is clean-shaven.

BLOW DRY FACTOR: Some impressive quiffs from the likes of George Kay. Admirable use of Brylcreem, many side partings and an early spiky flat-top from Billy Brown.

FAN FACTOR: Flat caps, trilbies, suits, ties, rattles, rosettes and giant hammers.

FLYING SO HIGH: WEST HAM'S CUP FINALS

ATTENDANCE: An estimated 200,000, plus the King and a white horse. Officially it was 126,067.

PRICE OF PROGRAMME: Three pence.

It's perhaps typical that West Ham should get to the club's first ever FA Cup Final and be upstaged by a horse. All that remains on film of the 1923 White Horse Cup Final is some grainy old footage of thousands of fans on the pitch and a voiceover by someone who sounds like Harry Enfield, yet it has entered popular folklore.

The 1923 FA Cup Final was the first game to be played at the newly-built Wembley. It provided a welcome distraction for working-class fans in a turbulent world.

The First World War had ended just five years earlier in 1918. Lenin had just stepped down as leader of the Soviet Union and the Nazi party held its first rally in Munich that January. The Prime Minister was Andrew Bonar Law, soon to be replaced by Stanley Baldwin. The first sound movie had been shown in New York. New legislation allowed wives to divorce faithless husbands. Though there was little chance of any saucy reading material, as James Joyce's new novel *Ulysses* had been banned in Britain.

The Empire Stadium, built by William McAlpine for the British Empire Exhibition of 1923, was only completed four days before the FA Cup Final. There was a strong suspicion the stadium wasn't properly ready and the perimeter defences appeared to be flimsy.

The final catches the imagination of the public. It's a clash between north and south. Underdogs West Ham are going for promotion from Division Two while Bolton are an established First Division side with star players like Jack and Vizard. And just five years after the carnage of the First World War it gives the poor, often-malnourished Eastenders, some hope.

Winger Jimmy Ruffell later commented: "It seemed like the most wonderful thing anyone had done... It was a hard time for most people around the East End. That was the best thing about it really; giving people, kids, something to smile about."

West Ham reach the final without facing any First Division opposition. The Irons beat Hull City, Brighton after a replay, Plymouth, and then Southampton in a second replay. In the semi-final at Stamford Bridge, Derby County are defeated 5-2 with Billy Brown and Billy Moore both scoring twice.

The *Stratford Express* describes Jimmy Ruffell as having "the fleetness of a deer" as he makes a goal for Brown. The *East Ham Echo* calls it "one of the finest displays of football seen in London for many a day" and emphasises that West Ham's five-man forward line has cost a mere £2000 between them.

Manager Syd King has a gift for PR and on the eve of the final is playing up West Ham's role as underdogs, saying that 20 years ago in 1903 the club was at the humble Memorial Ground and faced insolvency. Now West Ham is "on the threshold of the double" of promotion and an FA Cup victory.

West Ham United have a decent side. The legendary Vic Watson — set to become the club's record goal-scorer with 326 goals — is up front. He cost just £50 from Wellingborough in 1920 and will later gain five caps for England. Inside left Billy Moore is another fine striker who knows where the net is.

Goalkeeper Ted Hufton goes on to play 13 seasons for the club despite performing in what appears to be a chunky polo-necked sweater borrowed from polar explorer Ernest Shackleton. Skipper George Kay is a talented centre half signed from Belfast Celtic, who later goes on to manage Liverpool, where he wins the title in 1947.

Jimmy Ruffell is a "left wing flyer" to use the vernacular of the day, and eventually makes 548 appearances for the Irons. West Ham spotted him playing for the Ilford Electricity Works X1, a side no doubt packed with midfield dynamos.

The side has talented half-backs in Syd Bishop and Jack Tresadern. Above all, the lads have solid dependable names; characters called Syd, Jack, Billy, Dick and Ted will, like Billy Bonds, never let you down.

Before the match the West Ham players make a pre-match inspection of the Empire Stadium. In the old newsreel some of the players emerge on to the pitch puffing cigarettes and then pose for a team photo. There are no Liverpool-style white suits here, just heavy overcoats, round collared shirts, waistcoats, trilbies and unfeasibly large flat caps.

Footage also survives of a more relaxed photo-shoot of the side in their kit.

The programme has a pennant design on the cover and reflects the grandiosity of the occasion. It reads: "British Empire Exhibition Programme & Souvenir. Final Tie of the Football Association's English Cup Competition. To be played at The Empire Stadium Wembley April 28th 1923. Bolton Wanderers v West Ham United."

Wembley is a huge event for the East London fans. It's a perfect day and fans wishing to travel in style can take the train from Baker Street for one shilling. It's something of a pilgrimage with supporters setting off at dawn to walk to Wembley, even if they have the train fare.

In his excellent book *The Lads of '23*, Brian Belton interviews his grandfather, Jim, who walked to the game from Canning Town. Jim recalls meeting farm boys from Romford, Hornchurch and Dagenham, fishermen from Southend who had moored at Barking; Jewish lads from Bethnal Green and veterans from the Great War on crutches, all marching along waving model hammers.

Part of the problem on the day seems to be the pre-match hype in the press. Wembley is billed as the latest wonder of the world, a stadium so vast that it can cope with any number of fans that want to see the game and all of whom will have a perfect view. The *East Ham Echo* describes it as "the most wonderful sports arena in the world."

There's a lovely old photograph of a group of West Ham fans running towards the camera, arms aloft. They're wearing jackets and ties and flat caps and trilbies, but carrying the early signs of football fanatic paraphernalia. One is holding a replica FA Cup trophy above his head, another a rattle. There's a replica hammer, some have scarves and rosettes and there's a chirpy cockney type in a claret and blue top hat. Judging by the way they're performing for the camera it looks as if the odd pre-match beverage might have been partaken.

There's also newsreel footage of a suited fan with a bushy moustache standing by the twin towers. He's wearing a claret and blue hat and rosette and playfully wielding a giant hammer.

The official capacity of the new stadium is 125,000. But more than 200,000 fans arrive, most of them hoping to pay at the gate. In the old footage of the fans streaming off the trains, Wembley is surrounded by fields.

So many fans arriving causes consternation for the ill-prepared Wembley administrators and the *Daily Mail* later describes the stewarding as "useless." When the turnstiles are closed at 1.45pm, with some 125,000 fans already inside, the disappointed fans outside rush the gates. One of the main exits is broken down and the fans surge in, taking up seats that others have already paid for. It's so bad that one indignant member of the press complains that at least three quarters of those in the press box are gatecrashers.

A basic design flaw is that the turnstiles are outside the stadium and only a single storey high, easily scaled by a determined group of men, some of them war veterans. The *Times* estimates that around a thousand fans are injured trying to get inside.

What would today's media make of hundreds of thousands of people breaking into a football ground? The old film footage shows countless men in flat caps, some still carrying newspapers, standing on each other's shoulders and climbing over the perimeter walls.

Inside the stadium, the hoardings give way around the pitch and those at the front are pushed over the cinder track and on to the grass. The *Bolton Evening News* writes that, "in an incredibly short time the beautiful greensward was occupied by a black uncontrollable mass."

Most of those present are Londoners. West Ham trainer Charlie Paynter complained: "When the players of both sides got on the pitch there seemed quite a hundred London supporters to every Bolton supporter. My boys were slapped and pulled about, while the Bolton players got through practically unscathed."

In 2007 Sky Sports interviewed 92-year-old Denis Higham, who went to the Final from his Harrow home. Higham recalled: "When we got off the train there was no way of getting in the ground except to follow the crowd who were climbing the turnstiles. My dad, being fairly adventurous, said 'Come on lad; let's do what they're all doing.' So my dad and I actually got in without paying a penny!"

The mood was boisterous but helpful. When Higham was separated from his father someone shouted, "Look there's a young lad, let's give him a hand." He was lifted over the heads of the crowd and given a place near the front of the seething mass of humanity.

And some people are on the pitch… The police are powerless for a time, but eventually half a dozen mounted officers attempt to clear the playing surface.

At one stage it appears the match will be abandoned, but the presence of King George V is a key factor. His arrival produces an awesome chorus of *God Save the King* and many fans later describe it as one of the most moving moments of their lives. The King is said to have muttered solid British things like "Steady on boys!" as he sees the huge crowd. Perhaps fearing what an angry crowd might do if the game is abandoned, the police decide to clear the pitch and proceed with the game.

It's then that a horse takes over the final. Billie, the white (actually a grey) police horse gains immortality, as does his rider PC George Scorey. It helps that Billie stands out on the black and white newsreels too – in today's terms he is telegenic.

The *East Ham Echo* wrote: "Then came the miracle. Half a dozen mounted policemen arrived on the scene, and working from the centre of the pitch by great efforts, filched a little more space from the crowd, which the cordon of police endeavoured to hold… But wonders of wonders was the work of an inspector on a dashing white horse."

PC Scorey later explained: "The horse was very good – easing them back with his nose and tail until we got a goal-line cleared. I told them in front to join hands and heave and they went back step by step until we reached the line. Then they sat down and we went on like that... the horse seemed to understand what was required of him. The other helpful thing was the good nature of the crowd."

Eventually the pitch is cleared, but the fans are still cramped tightly on and sometimes over the touchlines. It's a struggle just to get on the pitch. Jimmy Ruffell has an injured shoulder that is aggravated by thousands of fans slapping him on the back. Jack Tresadern also receives "a severe shaking."

The game kicks off 43 minutes late, with the crowd on the touchline creating a peculiar, slightly menacing, claustrophobic atmosphere. The players are not sure if they are playing a friendly to placate the crowd, or whether it really is the final. Thousands of people can't see at all. One photograph shows several fans standing on the roof of the stand, having risked their lives shinning up a drainpipe. Amazingly no-one is killed.

Bolton are quicker to settle, having already experienced overcrowding problems in the semi-final victory over Sheffield United at Old Trafford. In a foretaste of West Ham's perennial ability to make life difficult for themselves, the Irons are a goal down after two minutes. West Ham's defender Jack Tresadern is still struggling to get back on to the pitch as David Jack scores, having found himself on he wrong side of the crowd on the touch-line. Jack's shot is so powerful it knocks out a spectator behind the goal, who then causes several others to fall.

FLYING SO HIGH: WEST HAM'S CUP FINALS

The normally reliable Vic Watson spurns a great chance when Bolton keeper Pym misses the ball. The *Times* writes: "How he managed to kick the ball over the cross-bar instead of into the net one cannot imagine; if a player tried to do it, the odds against him would be generous. Watson, however, did fail to score."

The crowd can easily trip up or impede a flying winger. If the fans are anything like the volume of today's vociferous supporters, it is surely a chastening experience for both sets of players. Whenever a player takes a corner the police have to move the crowds back so the player can take a run-up.

After 11 minutes the game has to be stopped after further encroachment and the pitch is cleared again. Fans are fainting on the pitch and being treated by the Red Cross, which is hardly conducive to a game of football.

At half-time the players are unable to leave the pitch. They are effectively prisoners and simply have a five-minute break where they stand. There is also the constant worry that such a large crowd, though good humoured for now, might turn riotous.

West Ham start the second half brightly. Pym almost fumbles Richards' shot over the line and Watson mishits a chance. But Bolton score again after 53 minutes. Vizard dribbles down the left and crosses for Jack Smith, who hits the crossbar with a powerful strike. It rebounds down on to the line and then back into play off a spectator. The ball is back in play so quickly that few fans realise that Smith had scored.

FLYING SO HIGH: WEST HAM'S CUP FINALS

Referee Mr Asson decrees that the ball has crossed the line and such is his authority, no West Ham players query the decision. Though clearly the lads have an early claim for the introduction of goal-line (or just any) technology. The Hammers players later complain that a Bolton fan has kicked the ball to Vizard during the move.

The game is a tepid affair for the final 30 minutes, descending into a series of fouls. Some fans drift away as it become obvious that the Cup is bound for Bolton. Captain George Kay tries to get the game abandoned, but Bolton captain Joe Smith tells the referee he is happy to play all night long.

The final whistle goes and the King presents the cup to Bolton's Joe Smith. Both sets of players attend a dinner afterwards and are presented with gold watches by former Prime Minister David Lloyd-George. In a bizarre postscript, PC Scorey is offered tickets to every future Cup Final by the FA, but refuses to go, as he doesn't like football.

Syd King is clearly upset after the game, tersely declaring: "I'm too disappointed to talk. I want to forget it." While trainer Charlie Paynter blames the Cup Final defeat on Billie the horse. He claims: "It was that white horse thumping its big feet into the pitch that made it hopeless. Our wingers Ruffell and Richards were tumbling all over the place, tripping up in great ruts and holes." A sound maxim for all gaffers: if in doubt blame the horse.

Paynter makes the reasonable point that the whole game was played in breach of FA Rule 5, which states that a player taking a throw-in must be behind the touchline: "It is pure imagination for anyone to say that the touchlines were clear. They were not."

The *East Ham Echo* reports: "There is talk of a protest to the FA against regarding the game as the FA Cup Final, but disappointed and dissatisfied as they must be with the West Ham directors, their team are too good sports to do that. Rule 5 states that the player making the throw-in has to be behind the touchline. This rarely happened during the game."

Good sports? Putting principles before results is to become a West Ham trait — this is, after all, the club that failed to sign Gordon Banks because Ron Greenwood had a gentleman's agreement to sign Bobby Ferguson.

The *Daily Mirror* devotes its front page to six pictures of the final including, "The King, accompanied by the Duke of Devonshire, gazing on the amazing scene." The *Mirror* hasn't quite mastered the art of the tabloid sensationalism though. One caption simply reads: "Butler putting the ball through for Bolton only to be given offside. Note crowd on goal-line."

What seems amazing today is that the event did not turn into a Hillsborough-type tragedy. As at Hillsborough, initially the authorities directed the fans into the lower pens first, rather than the comparatively unpacked upper tiers. Today's media might have concentrated less on British pluck and more on the fact that the fans forced their way in and that one thousand or so were injured.

Women were crushed against railings as the crowd stampeded and many fans fainted. Injuries recorded by local hospitals included broken arms and legs, abdominal injuries, crushed chests, and a man from Wisbech with an eye injury so serious that it might need to be removed. Had the fencing around the cinder track been stronger, or the crowd less good-humoured, or panic ensued, hundreds might have died.

As Jimmy Ruffell said in 1973: "We deserved to be in the final, Bolton and West Ham, but that everyone walked away from Wembley more or less in one piece was the biggest win of the day. People won the game really; more than either team."

In the aftermath of the match manager Syd King issues a statement. Possibly he is under pressure from his board, or perhaps he just wants to concentrate on the two league games yet to play, but he is keen to move on from the final:

"Although inundated with requests to lodge a protest against the result of the final tie, the directors of the West Ham club are satisfied that they were beaten by the better team on the day (under the conditions in which the match was played) but they do consider that the responsible officials of both clubs should have been informed at half-time as to whether the match was to be a Cup-tie or not; as in their opinion the match was not played under the rules of the FA (particularly with regard to Rule 5). Rule 5, deals with the conditions under which the ball shall be thrown from the touchline, but on Saturday the crowd were on the touchline practically all the time."

This is an interesting inference from West Ham, that the officials of both clubs "should have been informed at half-time as to whether the match was to be a Cup-tie or not." Could some players have believed that the final could not go ahead under such circumstances and that they were simply having a kick around just to keep the thousands happy?

It all seems very noble, but painfully stiff upper lip when compared to the bad sports of the modern era. Tottenham complained about a dodgy lasagne giving their side food poisoning when they lost at Upton Park in 2006 and Sheffield United were quick to go to litigation when it was claimed that Carlos Tevez was owned by a third party during the Hammers' 'Great Escape' season of 2006-07.

But in 1923 faced with thousands of extra fans obstructing the side's wingers, hoof marks and a game where no one was sure if was actually the final or a friendly to placate the crowd, West Ham refused to lodge any kind of protest.

Questions are later asked in the House of Commons. When Oswald Mosley, later to lead the British Union of Fascists, refers to "hooliganism", Alderman Jones, one of West Ham's MPs is most indignant, declaring: "If it had not been for the conduct of the police and the good humour of the crowd there would have been murder. Therefore, the Right Hon member for Harrow has no right to talk about hooliganism."

But never mind hooliganism, white horses and West Ham's keep calm and carry on stoicism; this is the year of the illuminated tram. Before the final it's been decided that win or lose the Irons will be rewarded with a ride in an illuminated tram to a civic reception on the Saturday night. It's the idea of Syd King and shows a flair for publicity ahead of his time. Hundreds of bulbs are used to create a crossed Hammers motif and a "Well done Hammers" sign on the side of the tram.

It travels down the tramlines from Canning Town along the Barking Road and Green Street to Stratford. Thousands of fans line the route. On Sunday there's another reception at East Ham and borough-wide parties, which probably lead to all those right old East End "cockney knees-up" clichés filtering their way into West Ham match reports ever since.

There's still league glory to follow. With two fixtures left to play, West Ham play Sheffield Wednesday away just 48 hours after the FA Cup Final. They win 2-0 with goals from Watson and Moore, but predictably the Irons then go and lose their final game at home to Notts County in front of 26,000 fans. Yet the fans' mood turns from despair to joy as the scoreboard reveals that West Ham have still gained promotion, finishing second on goal average as Leicester have lost at home to Bury.

Great years lie ahead. Except this being West Ham, in reality it's several mediocre seasons in the First Division. The club doesn't buy enough quality players and is eventually relegated in 1932. Tragically Syd King, who is well known in the local hostelries and used to send out young Ted Fenton, later to manage the Hammers, to get him crates of beer, is suspended for three months and then sacked, accused of being drunk and insubordinate at a board meeting. Nine days after his dismissal King commits suicide by drinking a mixture of "alcohol and a corrosive beverage."

But nothing can take away the glory of that 1923 Cup run and Syd King and West Ham's great moment, even if the game should never have been played. Perhaps a good lawyer could yet instigate a retrospective replay.

A game that was labelled a "Wembley fiasco" is perversely also one that will always be remembered.

The match had enough incident to keep John Motson in statistical anecdotes for perpetuity; a gleaming new stadium, fans breaking in, a near crowd disaster, a pitch invasion, the King, a telegenic horse, a contentious goal, fans fainting on the pitch, and claims that the match should be replayed because of constant encroachment by thousands of blokes in flat caps. West Ham have set a precedent. They might not get to Wembley very often, but when they do it's certainly memorable.

2. AND BOBBY MOORE HAS A GREAT BIG HAMMER!

1964 FA CUP FINAL

WEST HAM UNITED 3 PRESTON NORTH END 2

Wembley Stadium, Saturday May 2 1964. Kick-off 3pm.

WEST HAM: Jim Standen, John Bond, Ken Brown, Bobby Moore, Jack Burkett, Peter Brabrook, Eddie Bovington, Ronnie Boyce, John Sissons, Geoff Hurst, Johnny Byrne.

IF THE KITS ARE UNITED: Claret and blue shirts with shield-shaped badge of club crest, thigh-hugging white shorts and white socks.

FACIAL HAIR: Lots of youthful skin and a completely clean-shaven side.

BLOW DRY FACTOR: Ron Greenwood has a comb over, Ken Brown has a bit of a quiff, nice side partings from Geoff Hurst and John Sissons.

FAN FACTOR: Choruses of It's A Long Way To Tipperary and Bubbles. Suits, ties, plastic bowler hats, paper hats, rosettes, rattles, early banners and giant hammers.

FLYING SO HIGH: WEST HAM'S CUP FINALS

ATTENDANCE:100,000.

PRICE OF PROGRAMME: One shilling.

West Ham are at Wembley again, 41 years after the White Horse final. Football is on the cusp of a new era, changing from a game watched by men in suits and ties, to the scarves, chanting, exuberance and later hooliganism of the 1960s and 1970s.

The ads in the Wembley programme sum up the times; they're for cigarettes such as Senior Service Tipped and Woodbine Virginia, Schweppes lemonade and Booth's gin. "Double Diamond the beer real men drink," reads another advert over a picture of a mud-spattered jockey drinking DD from the bottle. While on the back cover two fans in scarves and caps are apparently from the "hot Bovril supporters club", drinking the "extracted goodness of prime lean beef." The fans are invited to "after the match drink your health in Bovril."

West Ham reach the Cup Final after a pulsating semi-final, beating Manchester United, the FA Cup holders, at Hillsborough. This is Sir Matt Busby's great team of Denis Law, George Best and Bobby Charlton. That 3-1 victory is surely the greatest triumph in the Hammers' history. The players have been angered by the media implying it will be easy for United. Then Ron Greenwood uses some motivational psychology. Having walked on to the pitch before the game he's found the Manchester United players warming up and laughing and joking with the Dagenham Girl Pipers. Greenwood goes back to the dressing room and tells his players: "Hey United think this is going to be easy. We've got a chance here!"

Ron 'Ticker' Boyce scores twice that afternoon, one from close on the halfway line. The decisive second goal comes from Geoff Hurst, after a great run and pass out of defence by the immaculate Bobby Moore. The pitch resembles a field trodden by a herd of cattle and the Hammers' famous light blue and claret hooped away kit is black with mud by the final whistle. The programme for the final has a picture captioned "The Hammers mudlark", showing John Bond with his arms aloft, his kit completely covered in mud.

Ron Greenwood manages to get left at the stadium talking to the BBC amid the celebrations, but catches up with the team at Sheffield station. The club had booked a dining car for the journey back to London but in the absence of security it is invaded by jubilant fans. Geoff Hurst describes the journey home as "madness" while Greenwood recalls the crush at the bar and that it was "like the January sales, Wembley Way and the London rush-hour rolled into one."

In the previous rounds the Hammers have beaten Charlton at home, Leyton Orient at Upton Park after a replay, Swindon away and Burnley at home.

And so on to Wembley, 1964. It's a time when Sir Alec-Douglas Home is Prime Minister, Dr Beeching is busy axing train lines and mods and rockers are fighting on the beach in Clacton. The

Great Train Robbers have just been sentenced. Actors Elizabeth Taylor and Richard Burton have married. William Hartnell is starring in a new science fiction series called *Doctor Who*. While the price of beer has risen after the budget to two shillings and one pence.

Before the Wembley final there's 'community singing' with Frank Rea, accompanied by the Band of the Welsh Guards, conducting the crowd in a swaying chorus of *It's a Long Way to Tipperary*. The Second World War has ended just 25 years earlier and the crowd respond with unbridled patriotism to the old song. The *Daily Express* song sheet reveals the fans are also invited to sing *Pack Up Your Troubles in Your Old Kit Bag*, *John Brown's Body*, *Underneath the Arches*, *She's A Lassie From Lancashire*, *Waltzing Matilda*, *Clementine* and of course, *Abide With Me*.

At the toss-up Bobby Moore jogs up to the centre spot with his distinctive springing gait and it's noticeable that he's wearing much shorter white shorts than his Preston counterpart, the ex-Manchester United player Nobby Lawson. This is a time when northern footballers have proper names like Nobby. The referee Arthur Holland has a vicious short back and sides, despite it being the 1960s, proving that no man in black has ever been fashionable.

Being only four at the time, this particular fan wasn't at the game, but it's still a great insight to watch the final. BBC commentator Kenneth Wolstenholme appears to be a man struggling with the rapid pace of sartorial change in the game.

24

"Both keepers are wearing gloves, very sensibly," he says of this new innovation. Though Ken appears baffled that West Ham keeper Jim Standen is wearing dark shorts while the rest of his side are wearing white shorts, and then he comments "You'll notice that on Standen's back he has the number one, he's the only goalkeeper in the league who wears a number." Whatever next? Names on shirts?

There's new-fangled tactics too. "Bobby Moore is the cover centre-half in the 4-2-4 system," explains Wolstenholme. Behind the goals the photographers are wearing Macs and suits, while the ball boys have skimpy shorts, white legs and trainers.

Early on Preston's 17-year-old Howard Kendall looks the best player on the pitch, showing no nerves and making many astute interceptions. Bobby Moore shows his class too. You notice how often he intercepts the ball before he needs to make a tackle and then sets up an attack with an accurate ball out of defence.

The pitch is rapidly covered in clumps of grass. "That's a mighty divot!" says Wolstenholme, admiringly, as Geoff Hurst's studs rip up a swathe of turf. It looks more like a surface suitable for the Grand National.

It's noticeable how quiet the crowd is. There are a few chants of "North End!" but the rest of it is just individual shouts and the odd cry of "Come on you Irons!" You can even hear the calls of the players.

Preston take the lead after ten minutes. Ross plays a long ball into the Hammers' box, bulky centre forward Dawson shoots from the edge of the area, Standen spills the ball and Holden scores from close in. Hammers' John Bond looks disconsolate on the line. "Well, the chips are down now!" exclaims Wolstenholme. The Preston fans in blue and white paper hats wave programmes and rattles in the air.

But two minutes later the Hammers equalise. Moore's ball forward is cleared by Preston. The ball falls to 18-year-old blonde winger John Sissons, who plays a speedy one-two with Johnny Byrne and despite the attentions of four defenders advancing towards him, fires low into the corner. It's a fine finish. You hear a roar from the Irons fans. "And it's the equaliser!" declares Wolstenholme.

The BBC cameras show some fans celebrating. They are hatless but all wearing jackets and ties. Many of them are smoking and one or two have rosettes on their jacket lapels. Sissons is hugged by Byrne and Burkett and holds both arms aloft in a child-like expression of joy. The Pathe Newsreel shows the West Ham end with primitive early banners, reading "Up the Hammers" and "West Ham United."

It's evident that the Hammers have been hustled out of their passing game by Preston. Sissons fluffs a cross and Brabrook takes a woeful corner. Wilson appears to have the beating of Burkett and Dawson is winning a lot of high balls against Brown.

FLYING SO HIGH: WEST HAM'S CUP FINALS

After 33 minutes comes the first chorus of *Bubbles*. It's slower and more melodic than the modern version, with a high-pitched tone to the collective voice. Wolstenholme notes the crowd is not swaying. Byrne finds Hurst who produces a fine save from Kelly. "They say they have to sway to score, they almost broke the rule there," adds Ken.

A neat summary of the manly attitude towards injury in 1960s football comes when Dawson goes down. "It would take a sledgehammer to knock him down and keep him down," Wolstenholme comments approvingly.

Disaster arrives on 40 minutes. The inspired Howard Kendall wins a corner and then comes the calamity defending. Standen slips on his goal-line and almost falls over, Ken Brown slips as he tries to challenge Dawson, and the man Wolstenholme describes as "a human missile" heads powerfully home. "A beautiful goal!"

The Hammers' wobble. Standen has to punch clear from Dawson and the big number nine then heads wide. Are West Ham going to blow their first trip to Wembley since 1923?

Half-time arrives and on march the Coldstream Guards Band, clad in bearskin hats and red jackets, playing rousing military fare. "It's a fair bet the Hammers have had a pep-talk at half time," suggests the plummy voice of the Pathe Newsreel commentary. Manager Ron Greenwood recalls in his autobiography *Sincerely Yours* that he'd been playing Bobby Moore as a sweeper, and felt he was being bypassed. So he moves Moore to a conventional centre back role and pushes Bovington into central midfield.

But still the passes are misplaced. On 51 minutes there's a fairly mournful version of *Bubbles* from the fans. Burkett hoofs the ball into the air and Wolstenholme comments, "Well that's not very distinguished sort of stuff is it?"

Thankfully the Hammers get back into the game quickly. In the 52nd minute Hurst chases a long ball and forces a corner. Brown heads on from the edge of the box and Hurst leaps high to head towards the net. Kelly saves it but the ball bounces off the prone keeper and over the line.

"Hurst has scored, the inside left!" declares Wolstenholme.

"It's time for a huggle!" suggests the Pathe Newsreel chap. Geoff gets a hair ruffle and a pat on the shoulder as he jogs back to centre circle in the understated style of 1960s goal celebrations.

West Ham play with a new intent. Bond fires a long ball into the mixer, Hurst heads, it's cleared back out by a defender to Bovington who fires just over. There's a big "Ooooh!" from the crowd.

In the Sam Allardyce era, it's interesting to note that back in the 1960s right-back John Bond frequently fires long balls into the box from near the half way line. Ron Greenwood's Academy could pass delightfully, but also mix it up too.

Boyce and Bovington start to win tackles in midfield. Hurst is possibly tripped when put through by Boyce. Preston reply, but Dawson shoots straight at Standen. On the hour a Hurst header from a Bond long ball is saved comfortably. The West Ham right back plays in another high ball and Byrne shows good control in the six-yard box, only to stub his boot in the muddy ground.

Still the pitch is cutting up. "Ken Brown must be a good golfer, he's just replaced a huge divot," remarks Wolstenholme. Preston's Holden fires just wide after last ditch Brown tackle.

Geoff Hurst just misses Brabrook's centre from the left and Wolstenholme implies he's a bit rubbish: "Ten thousand people wonder how Hurst managed to miss that." Sissons twists and turns past two defenders and his deflected shot almost bounces in off Kendall.

"And Singleton the Preston centre half has let his stockings come down," observes Wolstenholme, inspiring images of cross-dressing Sixties centre backs. "And he's discarded his shin pads, he may be feeling a wee bit of cramp."

When Preston do attack, Brown is winning more balls in the air against Lawton than he did in the first half. In a classic West Ham counter attack, Moore is on the touchline by his own goal but still finds Hurst with a superb ball. Byrne, Hurst and Brabrook combine and Hurst nods on the cross and Kelly saves low by post. You can hear a call of "give and go!" at Hurst during the build-up.

From a West Ham corner Boyce has a shot blocked and keeper Kelly is injured, taking a bang on the hip. There's another chorus of *Bubbles* while he's sponged down by the trainer. Back in those days we really did only have one song.

It's end to end. Wilson has a shot from the edge of the box saved at the second attempt and another effort easily fielded by Standen. Moore runs over the half way line to set up another move, but Bovington's cross is saved.

As the 90 minutes is up, "a lot of players have let their stockings roll down over their boot tops." Eddie Bovington becomes a victim of Wembley cramp and Kelly has more embrocation put on his hip.

It looks like extra time. But from Standen's goal kick, Hurst shows great control to pull the ball down, turn inside and run across the area. He's tackled but the ball breaks to Brabrook, who crosses. "Are we going to have a sensational ending – yes we are!" declares Wolstenholme as Ron Boyce arrives unmarked in the area to head the ball across the keeper and into the corner of the net.

Boyce runs behind the goal with his arms in the air and is hugged by Brabrook and Sissons. "Byrne is doing somersaults!" remarks Ken, while the Pathe Newsreel chap suggests, "Johnny Byrne starts a one-man training session." The cameras show West Ham fans arms in air, jumping up and down.

It's now forgotten, but the Irons almost concede an equalizer straight from the kick-off. Preston win a free kick on edge of box as Ashworth is brought down by Brown. Dawson's shot is deflected and there's a melee in the box, as the ball won't move, before finally being cleared. "I think I'd have given a set scrum for that," suggests the droll Mr Wolstenholme.

The whistle blows and West Ham have won the FA Cup for the first time. Sissons and Kendall embrace, as the youngest finalists salute each other.

The upright chap on the Pathe Newsreel commentary observes the embraces of the Hammers players and comes out with the pithy, "Serve them right if their best girls walk out on them!"

Bobby Moore walks up the steps to the Royal Box and receives the FA Cup from The Rt Hon the Earl of Harewood, President of the Football Association. The Pathe Newsreel catches an emotional chorus of *Bubbles* as he does so.

After the medals are presented the band play *God Save the Queen* as the players come down the steps and the defeated Preston players walk off. Bobby Moore is held shoulder-high by his teammates in front of the snappers. Bizarrely the band is still playing. Then it's the lap of honour as the Hammers fans celebrate wildly. "Well, all those bubbles they were blowing didn't fade and die," reflects Wolstenholme, "and Bobby Moore has a supporters banner, no it's a great big hammer!"

Moore and Byrne are running around the perimeter track with the giant hammer, with the words "WEST HAM FA CUP 1964" written on the top. "And Ken Brown has got a supporters hat on!" declares KW, astounded by the japes these modern footballers get up to, as the West Ham centre back dons a plastic claret and blue bowler. Eddie Bovington playfully pretends to hit Ken Brown on the head with the giant hammer.

"And a great swaying over to our left, *I'm Forever Blowing Bubbles* and a sight we've never seen at Wembley before," comments Wolstenholme. British restraint is lapsing and the West Ham fans are jumping up and down waving flags, loosening ties and going what in later years might be termed 'effing mental.

The BBC live coverage goes to a young David Coleman on the pitch, who grabs the players for a word into a giant microphone. Bobby Moore is as composed as you might expect and manages to find the right words amid the mayhem: "We got a lucky, well not a lucky goal but a good goal at the right time, David. We always felt that when we were behind we were likely to score goals, but we preferred it when we were in front. We had a quick chat at half time and tightened up a lot and we were more on top and we were more dominating."

Next up is Nobby Lawton the Preston captain and it's astonishing today to hear how sporting he is in defeat: "We gave West Ham a good game, but we're a bit disappointed at losing. West Ham deserved to win and they were the best team on the day. We gave them a good game but that's football…"

Ron Boyce tells Coleman: "It was just one of them things. I didn't have a good game all through and in the last minute it comes your way. He's been floating them over and I thought if I get in there there's a chance."

Referee Arthur Holland, about to retire, clearly finds questions about extra time from the young BBC upstart a little exasperating: "Well, there's got to be extra time, you want 90 minutes of football don't you? It was two minutes for the goalkeeper at the far end alone, you can't have 87 minutes, so extra time you've got to play!"

FLYING SO HIGH: WEST HAM'S CUP FINALS

Ron Greenwood has refused to be photographed holding the cup despite requests from his players, preferring instead to console Nobby Lawton. He's then accosted by Coleman, who suggests he must have been biting you nails towards the finish. "I don't bite my nails, I've lost my hair the lads have ruffled it up a little for me," answers Greenwood, looking like a benevolent house master.

When Coleman suggests he must have found it difficult to watch the later stages, Ron answers in typically philosophical fashion: "Well, all games are interesting to watch and it's our job to analyse and we can't afford to let emotions take over. At two-two I thought it could have gone either way, but luckily enough it went our way."

The Pathe Newsreel has footage inside the West Ham dressing room. It's full of photographers, which surely wouldn't be allowed today, and the players are drinking pints of milk. It's not simply that footballers were more wholesome in those days, this was part of a sponsorship deal with the National Dairy Council. "Never has the FA Cup been so misused!" quips the Pathe chap as the players drink milk from it and Ken Brown spills the white stuff down his shirt.

Saturday's *Evening News* runs the headline "London's Pride" and has a cut-out of Bobby Moore's head superimposed on a picture of the FA Cup. Monday's *Daily Mirror* credits West Ham's success to Greenwood's tactical changes with the headline: "The Master Stroke... Greenwood gambled — and turned the match."

After the final the victorious team have a 'do' at the Hilton hotel with 300 guests. One of the guests is Billy Moore from the 1923 West Ham Cup Final. In a nice piece of synchronicity it turns out that Ron Boyce's grandfather was a turnstile operator at that very White Horse Final. Ron Greenwood sleeps with the trophy under his bed.

The following morning the team take an open top bus from central London to the East End. Once they get to Petticoat Lane the whole of East London appeared to be on the streets. In *Sincerely Yours*, Greenwood sums up the moment: "Six miles of smiling faces, deafening cheers and waving banners. The lads and the Cup were on top. I sat inside relishing every second. All those lovely people were proof that our achievements mattered."

It's the club's first major trophy and a massive day in the East End. West Ham have arrived as a force in modern football.

And more Wembley glory is on the way...

3. CHAMPIONS OF EUROPE: THEY FLY SO HIGH, NEARLY REACH THE SKY...

1965 EUROPEAN CUP WINNERS' CUP FINAL

WEST HAM UNITED 2 TSV MUNICH 1860 0

Wembley Stadium, Wednesday May 19 1965. Kick-off 7.30pm.

WEST HAM: Jim Standen, Joe Kirkup, Jack Burkett, Martin Peters, Ken Brown, Bobby Moore, Alan Sealey, Ron Boyce, Geoff Hurst, Brian Dear.

IF THE KITS ARE UNITED: Claret and blue shirts with shield-shaped badge of club crest, white shorts, white socks.

FACIAL HAIR: Another clean-shaven bunch of lads without a hint of designer stubble.

BLOW DRY FACTOR: Nice blonde Barnets from Johnny Sissons and Bobby Moore, but generally it's still short back and sides and side-partings for these home boys.

FAN FACTOR: The first banners, jackets and ties, trilbies with badges and rosettes pinned to them, and the first West Ham pitch invaders since 1923.

FLYING SO HIGH: WEST HAM'S CUP FINALS

ATTENDANCE:100,000

PRICE OF PROGRAMME: One shilling.

A year after the FA Cup Final triumph, West Ham appear at Wembley again. European football has suited West Ham's technical game and their cerebral manager. Ron Greenwood, a long-time student of European football, has proved himself to be a great tactician, introducing such concepts as the deep-lying centre forward and five–man midfield long before they became fashionable.

In an epic run to the final of the Cup Winners' Cup, the side defeat La Gantoise, Spartak Prague, Lausanne and in the semi-final Real Zaragoza, winners of the Spanish Cup and the UEFA Cup. Having won 2-1 at Upton Park, in the away leg the Irons rely on a superb defensive performance from Bobby Moore and withdrawn roles for Hurst and Boyce. Having gone a goal down, John Sissons equalises after 54 minutes to send the 400 travelling Hammers fans into ecstasy and secure a 1-1 draw. The hardy away fans are pelted with cushions at the final whistle in a *Monty Python*-esque scenario of early 1960s aggro.

The only other English side to win a European trophy has been Bill Nicholson's Tottenham, two years previously. Can West Ham become the second?

It's an evolving Hammers side. Compared to the previous season's FA Cup winning line-up there are four changes, all of them on the right side of the team. Joe Kirkup has replaced John Bond at right-back, Martin Peters is in for Eddie Bovington and young goalscoring sensation Brian Dear replaces the injured Johnny Byrne.

Most crucially, right-winger Alan Sealey — the cousin of Les Sealey later to play in goal for Coventry City, Manchester United and West Ham — is favoured over Peter Brabrook. Sealey, a local lad from Canning Town, is known as Sammy to the rest of the players, a nickname derived from Sammy the Seal.

It's a particularly satisfying moment for Martin Peters who had been dropped for the 1964 FA Cup Final and knocked on the manager's door to complain. The West Ham manager was able to tease Peters before this game with the comment: "I thought you said I'd robbed you of your lifetime's ambition to play at Wembley?"

Fans on the train to Wembley peruse the *Evening News*, which has produced a cup special with the West Ham team picture on the front page as a salute to, "the homely team of Cockney kids from East London who have stunned the Continent with their skill and courage." The game sets a record for receipts for a floodlit match.

The Wembley programme has the same "Hot Bovril Supporters Club" advert that was in the 1964 FA Cup Final programme. And there's another "Double Diamond The Beer Men Drink" advert, this time with a mountaineer instead of a jockey knocking it back from the bottle. Men have advanced in the grooming stakes though: another product pushed is Yardley shower talc, that "dries between the toes... stops that sticky feeling... the mild deodorant gives that discreet confidence a man appreciates."

One advantage for West Ham is that Wembley was decided upon as the venue at the start of the season. Another boost is that the side had seen Munich play twice. Greenwood persuaded the side to see 1860 play Chelsea while on a European pre-season tour. And then with Wembley in mind, Greenwood insisted the side watched the semi-final Play-Off between Munich and Torino in Zurich. They sat on uncovered seats in a thunderstorm but gained a firm idea of the opposition's style. The only person missing was the manager himself, who was being confirmed in Loughton.

It's a balmy early summer's evening and it proves to be unforgettable for all those present. "That song of ours about bubbles seemed to fill the stadium," recalled Greenwood.

Before the game the Royal Artillery Band play songs from *South Pacific* and finish with the *Post Horn Gallop*, the horn solo that Alan Pardew resurrected for the 2004 Play-Off semi-final against Ipswich.

The atmosphere is vibrant and noisy. The Munich end is full of flags and according to commentator Kenneth Wolstenholme, "every hunting horn in Bavaria is here tonight!" Along with klaxons and a bell. The West Ham fans are mainly men in suits and ties, but with badges and rosettes pinned to trilbies. You see some of the first banners alongside Union Jacks. They're simple affairs, reading "Up the Hammers", "West Ham The Greatest" and just "West Ham" with crossed hammers underneath.

Watching the game again the first thing you notice is that whereas most games of this era appear slow, this seems very modern in its unrelenting pace. Jim Standen always rolls the ball out to a defender rather than kick it long and both sides are constantly seeking space and running off the ball in a game of constant counterattacking.

The main difference from the modern game is that no-one argues with the referee and players hand the ball back to the opposition when caught offside.

The first chance falls to West Ham. Brian Dear crosses and 19-year-old John Sissons pokes the ball wide of the post when he should score. Standen has to make a good block from Brunnenmeier and then Sissons plays in a great cross only for Sealey to miscue in front of goal.

The Munich goalkeeper Peter Radenkovic is clad in all-black and wearing a flat cap, which makes him look mysterious, foreign and a bit existential compared to green-clad Jim Standen. He has a brilliant game and throughout the 90 minutes the Munich fans regale him with chants of "Raddy! Raddy!"

The first chorus of *Bubbles* is audible after 24 minutes, a wafting sonorous melody of cockney voices immediately barracked by the Germans. As *Bubbles* fades BBC commentator Kenneth Wolstenholme spots something extraordinary on the touchline: "There's a sight you don't often see. There's a lady photographer behind the West Ham goal… Now why don't we have things like that at Wembley more often? Lovely blonde photographers like that make football a much better game."

The camera lingers on the blonde "lady photographer", who's wearing a white two-piece suit and heels and probably now makes art house films. When she later stops the ball Wolstenholme remarks: "She's a pretty good goalkeeper too isn't she?"

It's an absorbing first half, and ends with Raddy making another fine save from Dear's piledriver and both teams being applauded off.

The floodlights are on for the second half. Four minutes into the half, Martin Peters plays a fantastic through ball to John Sissons, bypassing four defenders. The young winger hits the post with a great effort from the edge of the box.

Indeed, Sissons is excellent throughout the game, showing a willingness to take on defenders and also shoot. You wonder why his career stalled at West Ham, Greenwood eventually selling him to Sheffield Wednesday five years later, amid mentions of 'family problems'. He should have been the fourth great player alongside Moore, Hurst and Peters.

Then comes a sustained spell of pressure from the quick-passing Munich side and Jim Standen makes three excellent close-range saves, first from Brunnenmeier and then using his feet to frustrate Grosser and Kuppers. West Ham rally and a Hurst rocket produces another brilliant save from the keeper.

The Hammers apply more pressure as Peters has a low shot saved and Sealey is brought down on the wing. Bobby Moore is almost a midfielder, orchestrating some great moves and at one point trying to chip Radenkovic. He plays in Hurst with a great ball but the keeper races out of his area taking, according to Wolstenholme, "huge steps like a kangaroo!"

Finally the breakthrough arrives after 69 minutes. Boyce makes a great interception in midfield and strides towards the Munich goal before playing in Sealey on the right edge of the area. The winger smashes a drive into the top corner of the net. Sealey turns a somersault in one of those unaffected celebrations typical of the Sixties and is then embraced by Kirkup and Peters.

The goal is also noticeable for possibly the first West Ham pitch invasion since 1923. "Sealey has scored! He's turning somersaults! And on to the pitch come some of the West Ham supporters!" declares Wolstenholme.

Sadly the BBC cameras are turned away from such nefarious behaviour so none of the invaders are immortalised in grainy black and white TV footage. The police soon clear the joyous supporters.

Two minutes later and the Hammers score again. It follows a professional foul by Raddy the keeper. He races outside his area to bring down Brian Dear. The players simply shake hands and there's no flourishing of imaginary cards or surrounding of the referee by irate players, as there would be today. But at least the Irons have a free kick.

The goal is the result of the many training ground hours that Greenwood's men spent rehearsing free-kicks. Geoff Hurst runs over the ball to confuse the defence, Bobby Moore chips the ball into the box to Martin Peters who has made a late run. Peters miscues the ball sideways, it deflects off a defender's leg and Alan Sealey lashes it home from close range. Sealey runs away punching the air. A photographer behind the goal jumps up and down too, suggesting that not all the snappers were disinterested journalists.

The rest of the game is a celebration for both the West Ham team and the fans. "We want three!" chant the terraces. John Sissons hits a tremendous effort against the bar from the edge of the area. Sissons misses in front of goal, Peters sets up Dear for an effort that's saved by Raddy's foot and Brian Dear has a goal disallowed, dubiously, for offside.

When Munich do attack Ken Brown intercepts. "This West Ham defence could stop an army of tanks!" exclaims Wolstenholme, a sentiment that has never again been applied to West Ham.

With ten minutes left the Hammers fans begin to sing "E-i-adio we've won the cup!" borrowing the song from Liverpool fans.

"The Mersey sound has obviously spread to the East of London!" declares Wolstenholme. The BBC recording of the game is a valuable time capsule of one commentator struggling to cope with huge changes as the sixties starts to swing. Lady photographers, pitch invasions, somersaulting footballers, horn-playing Germans and Merseybeat pop music... Whatever next? Men on the moon?

From only having one song the Hammers fans now have four as they chant "Sealey! Sealey!" It's *Bubbles* again, another save from Dear. Martin Peters tries to score with a bicycle kick and then it's all over. The West Ham players stand with their arms aloft. A mob of photographers rush on to the pitch with huge cameras. "And there's our blonde girlfriend, let's hope she gets a picture all to herself," says Wolstenholme.

The players walk up the steps to receive the trophy from Gustav Wiederkehr, the President of UEFA. *Bubbles* and "E-i-adio we've won the cup!" alternate among the fans. Bobby Moore immaculate as always, is followed by Ken Brown, Geoff Hurst, Alan Sealey and Ron Boyce. He takes the cup and hoists it up for the fans before kissing the trophy.

On the pitch the team hold up the trophy as the fans sing an emotional *I'm Forever Blowing Bubbles* and Moore is lifted shoulder high. It's at this moment that West Ham's reputation for entertaining football and producing something special under the lights is surely created.

True to his abstemious image, Ron Greenwood celebrates by sipping tea in the dressing room, saying, "This was our greatest game... a tremendous advertisement for football."

Incredibly this is Greenwood's first tilt at European football. As Geoff Hurst was to point out, it took Sir Matt Busby and Manchester United six attempts and Bill Shankly and Liverpool nine attempts to win their first European trophy. And all at a club invariably perceived to be 'homely' but not one of Europe or even England's giants.

A meal had been organised for the players and officials at the Wembley restaurant. Though as we saw with the 'lady photographer', women were not as yet welcomed in the sanctums of football. Ron Greenwood recalled that the wives and girlfriends were not included and he had to rush around getting them drinks and placating the understandably unhappy WAGs.

There is no official banquet as such, as Bobby Moore and the players had found the previous year's bash in a vast room at the Hilton too impersonal. Greenwood goes home to his wife Lucy while the players opt to go to their drinking dens of choice.

"Sealey (two goals in two mins) slams Germans!" is the *Daily Mirror's* nationalistic headline the next day. "West Ham's wonder triumph — all Europe sees what soccer can be!" Sealey's goals are captioned as "The clincher!" and "The sizzler!"

The *Mirror's* Ken Jones writes: "Hammers have been called fools and dreamers. Today they are the wise and brave. Conquerors of Munich, and of all those who doubted their ability and scoffed at their elegant skill."

He mentions that Sealey's wedding the previous Saturday was featured on German TV last week and that once again that millions of "Eurovision Soccer" TV viewers will have seen his two goals.

Jones is positively elegiac as he predicts that this was, "perhaps only the beginning of West Ham as they showed to all of Europe that elegant and imaginative football can also be successful." It wasn't of course, it would be another ten years and several relegation struggles before West Ham won another trophy.

The *Daily Express* has the headline: "NIGHT OF GLORY... Forever blowing bubbles... East End goes wild at Hammers' Cup victory."

The *Daily Telegraph* writes that the game is "a triumph for football itself" and says of West Ham's skipper: "Moore showed for 90 minutes the same strength of character as the little man who walked bravely up Wembley Way before the match blowing bagpipes. Courage of this sort builds empires, never mind about winning Cup Finals."

Another open top bus ride, accompanied by mounted policemen and motorcyclists, sees the players arriving at East Ham Town Hall, driving past an early Tesco that's next to a shop called Foodtown. A suited Bobby Moore holds the trophy up on the town hall balcony.

One sad postscript is the end of Alan Sealey's career. As if to emphasise the fleetingness of sporting success, in pre-season training that summer he trips over a wooden bench and breaks a leg while playing a game of cricket at West Ham's Chadwell Heath training ground. He never fully recovers and plays just four more times for West Ham, before moving to Plymouth and Romford. Sealey dies in 2006 from a heart attack, aged just 54.

These are not the days of great financial rewards for success. At the Newham Council civic reception for the side, the staff and players are presented with "inscribed table cigarette lighters." Yet the memories of an English club winning a European trophy at Wembley are incalculable to those who played.

It was possibly West Ham United's greatest triumph. Bobby Moore ranked it above the 1966 World Cup Final as his favourite match: "We had all come through the ranks. It was like winning the cup with your school team."

In *Yours Sincerely*, Greenwood, a committed Christian, used almost spiritual terms to describe the Munich game: "Three years of hard work and faith went into our win. Our principles were justified; we proved that football at its best is a game of beauty and intelligence. Players and ball were in happy harmony, while skill and method flourished together. Ideas and passes flowed. For me it was fulfilment."

It's a night when West Ham conquer Europe and win their second trophy in successive seasons. It is the epitome of Ron Greenwood's belief in pure football. Yet in some ways it also reveals the reasons for a ten-year-trophyless malaise. The only other trophy that West Ham won after 1965 was the 1966 World Cup Final, when eight other players, whose names I forget, aided Moore, Hurst and Peters as they beat West Germany 4-2.

From 1965 until 1970, when Martin Peters departed for Spurs, a side with three World Cup winners failed to win a trophy. Even after Peters left the drought continued until 1975.

In 1965, defensive stalwarts Jim Standen and Ken Brown were coming to the end of their careers and were never properly replaced. John Sissons didn't realise his potential and Ron Greenwood refused to compromise his attacking principles in the era of cynical win-at-all-costs teams like Leeds United. Northern teams relished playing a side that gave them so much space.

The players assumed there would be more nights of glory. Yet this European triumph was the summit of the Moore, Hurst and Peters era. And for one night at Wembley in May 1965 it was glorious.

4. TAYLOR MADE

1975 FA CUP FINAL

WEST HAM UNITED 2 FULHAM 0

Wembley Stadium, Saturday May 3 1975. Kick-off 3pm.

WEST HAM: Mervyn Day, John McDowell, Tommy Taylor, Kevin Lock, Frank Lampard, Pat Holland, Billy Bonds, Trevor Brooking, Graham Paddon, Billy Jennings, Alan Taylor. Substitute: Bobby Gould

IF THE KITS ARE UNITED: Claret and blue shirts with short sleeves and special Cup Final badge, white shorts and white socks.

FACIAL HAIR: Full beards sported by Billy Bonds, Graham Paddon and Frank Lampard. Impressive Onedin Line sideburns from Trevor Brooking.

BLOW DRY FACTOR: Billy Jennings' hair appears bigger than his whole body and remains in magnificent shape throughout the game. Graham Paddon has a blonde Silvikrin shine, Bonzo looks piratical and there's a 1950s quiff from John Lyall. Thomas Hardy agricultural labourer chic from tousled Tommy Taylor, pudding basin fringe from Kevin Lock.

FAN FACTOR: Silk scarves, new white scarves with claret and blue inlay, loon pants, Oxford Bags, white

49

coats, claret and blue top hats, plastic bowlers, Rubettes-style caps.

ATTENDANCE:100,000.

PRICE OF PROGRAMME: 20p

Ten years after winning the European Cup Winners' Cup the Hammers are back at Wembley. It's been a long wait. Bobby Moore has left a year earlier and in one of those great footballing ironies, is captaining West Ham's opponents, Second Division Fulham.

John Lyall is in his first season as team manager, with Ron Greenwood retained as general manager. Now there are new heroes for the Irons fans in Trevor Brooking, Billy Bonds and, for this season at least, Alan Taylor. Signed from lowly Rochdale for £45,000 in October, the speedy striker has helped turn the club's season around, along with fellow new signings Billy Jennings and Keith Robson.

West Ham have beaten Southampton at the Dell, Swindon in a replay at the County Ground and QPR at home through Keith Robson's winner. Then Lyall introduces 21-year-old Taylor to the side for the quarter final at Arsenal watched by 56,000 fans. His first goal on a quagmire of a pitch is a tap-in from Paddon's cross and causes a huge surge from the West Ham fans illicitly standing in the Arsenal North Bank. Taylor's second comes near the end, following a Brooking one-two and a fine placed finish.

The first semi-final at Villa Park is a dull goalless draw. But the replay is at Stamford Bridge, and thousands of Irons fans make their way down the District Line. Before the game the PA plays *I Can Do It* by the Rubettes, who are Hammers fans, which seems prophetic to this supporter standing in the West Ham end. West Ham take the lead when Taylor heads in a left-wing cross from one yard out. Ipswich equalise through a sliced own goal from Billy Jennings and then have two goals disallowed by ref Clive Thomas.

It's a bizarre night weather-wise with snow swirling around the pitch at one point. But with a few minutes remaining Taylor races on to a clearance on the edge of the box and fires home to notch another double. It sends the hordes at the open end of Stamford Bridge into delirium and sets up a "Cockney Final" against Fulham, who that same evening have beaten Birmingham in their own replay.

After beating Ipswich the players record a single of *I'm Forever Blowing Bubbles*. It's still played before home games today and in 2012 the *Guardian* cited it as one of the greatest football songs ever recorded. There's a fine picture of the lads in the studio wearing classic 1970s football gear. Graham Paddon is in a black leather jacket and orange and green psychedelic shirt, Frank Lampard Senior is clad in a silk shirt, Kevin Lock has an iffy brown patterned jumper and John McDowell is wearing an equally dodgy brown

51

cardigan. Tommy Taylor, Alan Taylor and Bobby Gould are in wide-collared shirts that look as if they were purchased from Mr Byrite in Romford.

West Ham switch off in the league, only winning one of their final nine games and then it's on to Wembley. In May 1975 Harold Wilson is the Prime Minister and Margaret Thatcher is the new Conservative leader. The Cabinet is split on staying in the Common Market, unemployment has just hit one million, and the IRA is still active in London. British Leyland is about to be nationalised, Mud are number one in the charts with *Oh Boy* and Tom Baker is on *Doctor Who* in the story *Revenge of the Cybermen* that very night.

Inside Wembley the West Ham fans have many more scarves and banners than in 1964 and 1965. The banners are home-made affairs daubed on white sheets with plenty of crossed hammers and slogans such as "It's Mervyn's Day", "Billy Bites Balls" and "Lyall's Kings."

This was my first Cup Final, attended with a silk scarf around my wrist, and for a 15-year-old boy the noise the banners and the atmosphere was unforgettable.

The programme has an advert for Player's No 6 on the back cover and on the inside back cover a pint of Double Diamond in a DD glass tankard, with the slogan: "Just when you need it." Other adverts induce the fans to buy Castella cigars and Power football boots. Souvenir Cup Final records are £2.30 and 8mm soccer films £4.95 and a projector is £13.75 from Quality Products in Romford.

FLYING SO HIGH: WEST HAM'S CUP FINALS

Billy Bonds and his West Ham side walk on to the pitch in their new Bukta short-sleeve claret and blue shirts with a special 1975 FA Cup Final badge on the chest. This is the era when substitutes are never tracksuited; instead West Ham's twelfth man Bobby Gould has a green sweatshirt on.

The players are led out by team manager John Lyall, with general manager Ron Greenwood sitting on the bench, despite some talk that they would lead the side out together. Greenwood was clear that the honour should go to the team manager.

John Lyall looks purposeful in his suit with his firm jaw, dark hair and hint of a quiff. He's actually quite a young man for a gaffer. His playing career was cut short by injury and Johnny Lyall is just 35-years-old

After a legal wrangle Fulham have had to black out all markings on their boots, but in a daringly modern concession to fashion arrive with white tracksuit tops on, with each player's name written on the back. They are lead out by Alec Stock, later to be the prototype for *The Fast Show's* Ron Manager.

There's a huge chorus of *Bubbles* from the fans as Billy Bonds introduces HRH The Duke of Edinburgh to his side. And then, to the tune of *Amazing Grace*, a rendition of the mantra, "Lyall...Lyall...Lyall..."

The bearded Billy Bonds looks like he could be a bass player for a mid-seventies prog rock group. On the ITV commentary, Brian Moore is quick to get in his first reference to "buccaneering Billy Bonds" even before the game has kicked off.

Moore also mentions that Mervyn Day is just 19 and playing in the Cup Final. He's wearing one of those 1970s green goalkeeping shirts with a triangular collar.

Kevin Lock is another young Hammers star to make the line-up, aged just 21 and billed as "the new Bobby Moore", despite having a pudding-basin fringe, a crime against style that the fastidious Mooro would never have allowed his unisex hairdresser to contemplate.

The reliable Pat Holland is in for the injured Keith Robson. The loss of Robbo is a blow for the Hammers, a skilful but aggressive bearded Geordie. He brought real aggression to the Hammers left flank and as a bonus for the fans he was a bit of a nutter too.

What's often forgotten about this game is how much Fulham dominate the first half. West Ham look terribly nervous from the start. John Mitchell heads wide from a Bobby Moore free kick after a couple of minutes and then a bad clearance from Kevin Lock results in a swerving shot from Alan Slough that Day does well to hold.

Barrett heads wide across the Irons' goal, gangling centre-back John Lacy heads just past the post from a Fulham corner. Busby has an effort saved by Day and soon Lacy wins another ball in the box to cause a scare. "West Ham are all over the place," comments Brian Moore. "Come on you whites!" chant the Fulham fans.

Watching the final today the hoardings provide much interest and it's amusing to see tackles going in in front of a giant Rizla sign. Other adverts are for Esso Uniflo, Chessington Zoo, Dulux paint and Joe Coral. The ball boys have the word "ADMIRAL" on the front of their grey track suits while the photographers are a mix of balding blokes in suits and bad glasses and youngsters with Bay City Rollers haircuts.

With half an hour gone it's been all Fulham, with just one West Ham corner and veteran Alan Mullery, Conway and Slough dominating midfield. Bobby Moore is sweeping up everything at the back for Fulham and makes one brilliant interception to foil Brooking.

Kevin Lock makes a couple of excellent tackles, but the side just isn't playing. Billy Bonds is still restricted by a groin problem, Paddon isn't getting down the left flank, Tommy Taylor looks erratic, the full-backs are stretched and the midfield isn't involved. Alan Taylor barely gets a touch and only Billy Jennings provides any sort of threat up front.

There's a slow chorus of *Bubbles* from the fans which sounds almost like a lament as West Ham appear to be about to lose to a Second Division side. On the bench Ron Greenwood and John Lyall look perplexed. Physio Rob Jenkins is wearing a day-glow blue tracksuit that looks like it was purchased from the Green Street market and has a yellow Gola bag, a bucket and magic sponge in front of him.

Things are so bad after half an hour Billy Bonds rolls his socks down and plays the rest of the game without shin guards, something that would never be allowed in the modern game. He has the casual look of a bloke playing five-a-side. Though as an opposition player you'd be pretty scared of tapping Billy's unguarded shins.

The Hammers' few moments of class come from Trevor Brooking when he lets the ball run past defenders to bamboozle them or gets a cross in with no backlift. His dangerous cross reaches Jennings who can't quite lift his header over keeper Peter Mellor.

Towards the end of the half the Hammers show some signs of life. McDowell blazes a wild shot in the direction of Harrow. Brooking finds Billy Bonds with a fine ball but Mellor smothers the danger. Trev then chips a great ball to Bonds in the box, but Billy's volley balloons over the bar. Paddon's free kick is headed over the bar by Taylor.

Half-time arrives and on come the red-uniformed Massed Bands of the Royal Corps of Engineers, looking strangely anachronistic, even in 1975. Lyall and Greenwood urge Paddon and Holland to get down the left flank. As the players emerge for the second half Mervyn Day is joking with a Fulham player, something you can't imagine happening today.

There's a portent of future events when McDowell shoots hard and low and Mellor spills the ball, with Alan Taylor almost getting the rebound. But Bobby Moore is still imperious at the back, at one point nearly setting Busby away with a great long ball from the back. He's 34, a little portlier, but still looks capable of playing at the top level; you wonder why West Ham sold him in 1974. His place went to first Mick McGiven and then

Kevin Lock, but surely a player of Moore's class could have gone on much longer?

Fulham very nearly take the lead when Mitchell turns Lock on the right hand side of the box and volleys at goal only for Day to push the ball away for a corner. Graham Paddon rolls his socks down and starts to get down the left wing more.

On the ITV Sport coverage, which seems to be unashamedly biased towards the underdogs, Alan Ball announces that, "West Ham are there for the taking!" Thankfully this evokes the commentator's curse of such pronouncements making you look like a right plonker when exactly the opposite reaction occurs.

"But maybe it's West Ham who will be doing the taking…" suggests Brian Moore, as Pat Holland dispossesses Cutbush on the left side of the pitch, not far over the half-way line. Holland advances and plays the ball inside to Billy Jennings who shoots hard and low. Mellor parties the shot, but it comes off him to Taylor on the right of the six-yard box and the man the lads nicknamed 'Sparrer' after his thin legs and 'Whippet' because of his speed, shoots through the legs of the hapless custodian and into the net.

You can see the odd West Ham fan jumping up and down behind the Fulham goal, while the terraces at the other end of the stadium erupt in a sea of surging and jumping and fist shaking.

On ITV Brian Moore is exclaiming: "Mellor gets it… Taylor turns it back. Yes! Alan Taylor! One-nil West Ham! Against the run of play the side that has been on the receiving end for all the first half and a good percentage of the second makes the breakthrough… and there's a man who six months ago was playing in front of a handful of people for Rochdale! You can only feel sorry for Fulham… and the *Bubbles* song can be heard all around Wembley Stadium!"

On the BBC David Coleman is a little more prosaic: "Jennings… Alan Taylor! Right through Peter Mellor!"

Taylor runs away with two arms in the air and is lifted-up by Billy Bonds as the team form a group hug. Billy Jennings gives Pat Holland a piggy-back.

The West Ham fans raise an impressive chorus of *Bubbles* and then "And now you're gonna believe us, we're gonna win the cup!"

The cameras show a swaying, jumping mass of humanity, brandishing banners and a replica cup, with blokes in white coats on people's shoulders, lots of hats and scarves held up above heads and stretched between people's hands. On ITV Brian Moore dips into his Cockney patois repertoire to suggest, "There will be a few knees-up in the old East End tonight."

Four minutes later Taylor strikes again. Billy Bonds starts the attack with a run down the right flank. Lampard scuffs a shot, and the ball comes to Paddon, then Holland on the left. The underrated Holland jinks a lovely ball between two defenders and in to the path of Paddon who fires a powerful drive at Mellor. The Fulham keeper gets in a hopeless tangle parrying the ball, trying to kick it away with a flailing leg and watching Taylor prod it into the roof of the net.

FLYING SO HIGH: WEST HAM'S CUP FINALS

Brian Moore exclaims: "And hit well by Paddon! Number two! And he's done it again! Alan Taylor! Two goals in the quarter final, two goals in the semi final and two goals in the final!"

On the BBC David Coleman goes into statistical and literary overdrive: "And Taylor again! And Alan Taylor gets his sixth goal in FA Cup football in three rounds! Sixty-five minutes, two goals in four minutes and no one would dare write a story like this even in a fictional world!"

For the rest of the match the West Ham fans give a masterclass in pre-all-seater stadia raucous singing: *Bubbles*, "Lyall… Lyall…" again, "We want three!" and *You'll Never Walk Alone,* back in the time when all fans sang it and not just Liverpool supporters.

Fulham aren't finished though. A rebound off Lock lets in Mitchell for a one-on-one with Mervyn Day and the keeper saves with a combination of hands, chest and foot. "La la la la la la la… West Ham!" sing the fans. West Ham have confidence now as Fulham tire. Paddon volleys just over and then Paddon sets up Lampard, who finally connects well and has a trademark shot tipped away from the top corner by Mellor.

There's a lovely moment five minutes from the end when Frank Lampard attempts to nutmeg Bobby Moore. He fails and Moore stands grinning with the ball before imperiously flicking it away to a colleague. Football seems friendlier and no doubt Frank and Bobby share a Double Diamond after the game.

West Ham have to rely on a professional foul by John McDowell a few minutes from the end. He pulls back Les Barrett by the shoulder on the edge of the box. In 1975 McDowell doesn't even receive a yellow card, though Brian Moore does exclaim, "Oh, a bad challenge by McDowell, they might be a little annoyed by that."

Towards the end the Irons fans serenade the side with "Easy! Easy!" and "E-i-adio We've won the Cup!"

Referee Pat Partridge blows the final whistle to a huge cheer. West Ham have won the FA Cup for the second time in their history. John Lyall and Ron Greenwood embrace on the bench. Men with giant cameras rush on the pitch. Sub Bobby Gould looks rightly fed up that he hasn't been allowed a run-out for the last five minutes.

Alan Taylor embraces Billy Bonds and gives Bobby Moore a hug. The snappers gather round the former West Ham skipper. A West Ham fan carrying a giant hammer, clad in a white jacket with "Super Hammers" written on the back and wearing trousers with one claret leg and one blue leg, runs on the pitch to shake Moore by the hand and give him a hug.

As the players wait to go up to the Royal Box young Mervyn Day wipes away a tear and is hugged by Lyall. Alan Taylor is waving a silk West Ham scarf as they go up the steps and Bobby Gould finally gets to take off his green sweatshirt.

Billy Bonds gets his hair ruffled by young fans in claret and blue bowlers and receives the cup from HRH the Duke of Kent. He lifts the trophy with a big grin. With the bearded Lampard behind him it looks like an outtake of *Pirates of the Caribbean* as they lift their booty and Tommy Taylor lingers behind like an old tousle-haired sea dog.

And then comes the pitch invasion from West Ham fans. "And for the first time since I've been at Wembley there's been a pitch invasion, They'll have to get off," says a disproving Brian Moore.

My abiding memory of the game is Trevor Brooking wearing a claret and blue top hat and being carried shoulder-high around the ground during the team's chaotic lap of honour. FA Secretary Ted Croker and Ron Greenwood had to ask over the PA for the pitch to be cleared so West Ham could complete their lap of honour.

The surviving footage shows numerous youths in voluminous flared denims and t-shirts with flags draped over their shoulders standing before a banner reading "It's Mervyn's Day." A bloke in a white lab coat is confidently walking away with what appears to be the corner flag. Billy Jennings wears a scarf and is being chaired by youths with Paul McCartney Barnets and mutton-chop sideburns.

John Lyall is quick to defend the West Ham fans' invasion as only over-enthusiasm, though it's a pointer to the way football is heading.

After the match Lyall singles out Greenwood and Pat Holland for special praise: "We all owe a lot of credit to Ron Greenwood, that's the sentimental part of it for us. He has kept on the sidelines as he always would do and we all owe a tremendous debt to him... Pat Holland did a tremendous job out there, as did all the lads, but he was the one who had to come in and was under pressure."

"2-goal Alan wins Knees-up Cup!" reads the front page of the next day's *Sunday Mirror*. "Tinker Taylor!… Royal box knees-up," is the heading for the match report, next to a "Cockney Cup Final" graphic. Never slow to use one regional stereotype when two will do, the *Mirror* headlines another feature "Ee, bah gum" to describe the rise of Taylor from playing at Rochdale. "Now London belongs to this 21-year-old Lancashire hot pot."

Though one of the most poignant newspaper photos is of Bobby Moore leaving the pitch, virtually ignored in all the celebratory mayhem.

Sunday's five-mile open-top bus ride through East London is described by the *Sun* as "Up the 'Ammers!" and "It's V-E13 day for Fans." The feature is accompanied by a picture of Billy Jennings holding a bottle of beer and the FA Cup outside Newham Town Hall.

Some 250,000 fans line the route, though the *Sun* notes that Alan Taylor prefers lemonade to beer, unlike the rest of the players. On the balcony Billy Bonds has his shirt collars outside his leather jacket while Trevor Brooking opts for the trendy antique dealer look of a polo-neck sweater and double-breasted jacket.

West Ham have a trophy again after a decade-long wait and the Irons are back in the European Cup Winners' Cup. Under John Lyall there's real hope that the side will add steel to the skill of the Greenwood years.

5. BUT ROBSON WAS ON HIS KNEES TO HEAD IT IN!

1976 EUROPEAN CUP WINNERS' CUP FINAL

ANDERLECHT 4 WEST HAM UNITED 2

Heysel Stadium, Brussels, Wednesday May 5 1976. Kick-off 7.30pm

WEST HAM LINE-UP: Mervyn Day; Keith Coleman, Tommy Taylor, Billy Bonds, Frank Lampard, (Alan Taylor, 46 mins); Pat Holland, Trevor Brooking, John McDowell, Graham Paddon; Billy Jennings, Keith Robson. Unused substitutes: Bobby Ferguson, Kevin Lock, Alan Curbishley.

IF THE KITS ARE UNITED: Classic Admiral kit with v-shaped wedge of blue above claret shirt and four v-shaped lines across the front and winged blue collars. White shorts and socks.

FACIAL HAIR: Keith Robson has a northerner's moustache; Frank Lampard has his trusty beard as does Billy Bonds.

BLOW DRY FACTOR: Billy Jennings rules supreme again, while Graham Paddon has very well shampooed

65

blonde hair.

FAN FACTOR: White West Ham flags with crossed hammers, silk scarves, loon pants, passports and lots of bottles of duty-free Belgian lager.

ATTENDANCE: 58,000

PRICE OF PROGRAMME: 25f

A year after beating Fulham at Wembley West Ham have reached the European Cup Winners' Cup Final after some epic performances. In earlier rounds John Lyall's men overcame Lahden Reipas from Finland and Russian side Ararat Erevan.

In the quarter-final they were in serious trouble after going 4-0 down at half-time in the away leg at Den Haag. Luckily Billy Jennings pulled back a couple of goals in the second half to make it a 4-2 defeat. The odds were still against West Ham at Upton Park, but thanks to goals from Alan Taylor, Lampard (a 30-yard special into the top corner) and Bonds, the Hammers pull off a great comeback.

The semi-final against Eintracht Frankfurt produces one of the greatest European nights at Upton Park. West Ham are 2-1 down after the away leg, with Graham Paddon having scored the Hammers' goal in that game. The Boleyn Ground is full of 39,202 expectant fans for the second leg. After a goalless first half the crowd are not to be disappointed as Lampard crosses and Trevor

Brooking rises high in the muddy goalmouth to score with an unusually emphatic header.

The key moment arrives in the 67th minute. Brooking finds Keith Robson with a great first-time ball out to the left. I'm standing in the South Bank while the crowd groan as instead of advancing on goal Robbo turn backwards. But thirty yards from goal he pirouettes to whack a thunderous left shot into the top corner of the net for his first goal since November. "Oh but he let it go a yard too far… oh but a great goal!" is Brian Moore's memorable response on the ITV commentary.

West Ham's third is even better. Taylor plays a long ball through to Brooking, who turns inside an Eintracht defender with a beautiful dummy, sending the German somewhere towards East Ham station, before calmly stroking the ball home. Trev runs to the West Stand with one arm in the air. "Yes number three, magnificent!" shouts Brian Moore, sounding like the most excitable man on the planet.

As a chorus of *Bubbles* wafts over Upton Park Eintracht pull one back in the 87th minute, but the Irons' hold on for a memorable 4-3 aggregate victory. After watching the game and returning home on the District line I enjoy a particularly satisfying pint of bitter in the Essex Yeoman by Upminster station.

So West Ham are in their second successive Cup Final, having beaten Fulham at Wembley in 1975. Yet the glorious European nights also mask a terrible post-Christmas decline in league form. After beating Eintracht they are walloped 6-1 in a total capitulation at Arsenal. Incredibly West Ham don't win any of their final 16 league matches, taking just six points. As the *Hammer* programme later puts it: "Our eventual position in the table was incontroversial evidence of the general decline which befell us in the later half of the campaign."

The Final is going to be played at Brussels in the Heysel stadium — later to become infamous after the death of 39 fans at the 1985 European Cup Final — giving Belgian Cup Winners Anderlecht the advantage of playing in their home country.

For a time I think about going, even getting a temporary passport from Brentwood Post Office. But ultimately my sixth-former's budget and the fact that I've never been abroad before and it seems quite scary, means that this not-very cosmopolitan 16-year-old fan watches it live at home on the BBC, with David Coleman doing the commentary.

Some ten thousand Hammers fans have made their way on ferries and planes to Belgium. Inside the Heysel stadium it has decidedly Anglo-Saxon advertising hoardings promoting Intersport, Timex, Kent and Texaco. The Irons are playing in a posh new Admiral kit with modern colours and v-shaped bands of claret on the blue part of their shirts. West Ham settle quite quickly and so do the fans, with lager-fortified choruses of *I'm Forever Blowing Bubble*s clearly audible on my TV.

Billy Jennings shoots over and then troubles the keeper with a looping header. From the resulting corner West Ham score after 28 minutes. The short corner is played to Paddon who lofts a high ball into the box. Bonds wins the header, knocking it down for Patsy Holland, nipping into the box, to poke past

68

Ruiter. "Yes, Holland, one-nil!" declares Coleman with his customary brevity.

Not untypically, West Ham then concede an equaliser just before half-time. From near the touchline Frank Lampard underhits a back-pass to Mervyn Day. It turns into a perfect ball for the number nine Ressel, who passes across the box to Rob Rensenbrink. Billy Bonds gets a toe to the ball and almost makes a saving tackle, but Rensenbrink rounds the fallen Bonzo to fire into the net past a despairing Day and Tommy Taylor on the line.

David Coleman comments: "Frank Lampard walks away as Anderlecht celebrate a really gift goal... he looks the loneliest man in the ground." Lampard is later to blame his back pass on his studs catching in the long grass. Poor old Frank also manages to aggravate his groin injury playing that back pass and has to be replaced by Alan Taylor at half-time.

It gets worse. Three minutes after half-time Rensenbrink breaks at speed and finds Francois Van der Elst (later to play for West Ham) on the right of the box. He effortlessly cuts inside Tommy Taylor and curls a lovely shot into the top of the goal. A classic Colemanballs follows as David confidently says "One-nil!" before correcting himself, "Two-one, Van der Elst got it... West Ham pulled apart!"

But West Ham have enough spirit to fight back. When a corner is headed out by a defender Tommy Taylor produces the greatest shot of his career, a thumping volley that Ruiter somehow tips away from the top corner.

The equaliser comes after 69 minutes when McDowell finds Brooking, who crosses from the left. Keith Robson stoops to send a delightful glancing header in off the post. Robbo runs to the flag-waving West Ham fans and I jump out of my armchair at home. "But Robson was on his knees to head it in!" declares an agitated David Coleman.

Sadly West Ham's lead only last four minutes. Mervyn Day has to make a smart stop from Vercauteren and then rush from his line to deny Van der Elst. In another wave of Anderlecht attacking the ball is in and around West Ham's area for a minute or so with no-one able to make a decisive clearance. Eventually the ball falls to Rensenbrink on the left, Pat Holland lunges for the ball and plays the man. Penalty, despite the protests from Billy Bonds to the French referee Wurtz. The ubiquitous Rensenbrink fires straight down the middle and over the diving Day.

Day makes another good stop from Van der Elst. West Ham's best chance of an equaliser comes when Jennings heads wide from a decent Brooking cross.

It's all over after 85 minutes. Pushing upfield West Ham are undone when Rensenbrink, emerging from his own half, finds Van der Elst running at the retreating defence. The Dutchman turns McDowell one way then another and leaves Day on the ground as he strokes home a lovely goal. "West Ham's all out attempt to attack was caught then... with the defence caught pushing forwards and square," intones David Coleman. All that's left is the handshakes at the final whistle.

70

As I head for my Dad's home brew I'm disheartened, but also proud of the lads. We've done well against a side playing in their home country featuring major talents in Rensenbrink, Van Der Elst and Haan. As John Lyall later wrote in *Just Like My Dreams*: "It had been a marvellous match, full of skill and passion, and a fitting climax to a season that had promised much for so long." And surely there will be more European finals to come.

6. TREVOR BROOKING WALKS ON WATER...

1980 FA CUP FINAL

WEST HAM UNITED 1 ARSENAL 0

Wembley Stadium, Saturday May 10 1980. Kick-off 3pm.

WEST HAM: Phil Parkes, Ray Stewart, Alvin Martin, Billy Bonds, Frank Lampard, Geoff Pike, Paul Allen, Trevor Brooking, Alan Devonshire, Stuart Pearson, David Cross. Substitute: Paul Brush

IF THE KITS ARE UNITED: All white Admiral away kit with light blue trimmings and claret stripes on collars and shorts.

FACIAL HAIR: Full beards sported by David 'Psycho' Cross and Frank Lampard. A 'seventies porn star' moustache from Phil Parkes and a 'fifties cad' moustache from Alan Devonshire.

BLOW DRY FACTOR: Phil Parkes has that Cossack natural hair control sheen to his fair locks, Billy Bonds has shaved his beard off and has similarly shiny hair, while Alvin Martin simply has hair, which is a novelty.

73

FLYING SO HIGH: WEST HAM'S CUP FINALS

FAN FACTOR: The first commercially made West Ham flags, white scarves with claret and blue banding, Admiral shirts, claret and blue rugby shirts and white and claret baggy caps.

ATTENDANCE:100,000.

PRICE OF PROGRAMME: 80p

How did West Ham reach the 1980 FA Cup Final? There's a song about that. It goes: "I'm dreaming of a Frank Lampard/Just like the one at Elland Road/When the ball came over and Frank fell over and scored the f***ing winning goal!"

The first semi-final at Villa Park has ended in a 1-1 draw with Stuart Pearson equalising Brian Kidd's penalty. In the replay at Elland Road it's goalless after 90 minutes. Alan Devonshire puts the Hammers ahead after a brilliant solo dribble. Bob Latchford levels the scores after 113 minutes, scoring with a glancing header and leaping on to the fencing to celebrate with the Everton fans.

With just two minutes to go, Brooking swings over a cross, David Cross nods on and there in the box is left back Frank Lampard, diving full length to score the unlikeliest of winners. His celebration goes into West Ham folklore as the left back runs dementedly round the corner flag in an early version of pole dancing for bearded blokes.

When West Ham are drawn away to West Brom in the third round of the cup I'm returning in my friend Will's car after watching the Irons lose 3-0 at Shrewsbury. "That's us out then," we agree. But Phil Parkes plays one of the best games of his life to earn a draw and West Ham win the replay at Upton Park.

In the next game the Hammers win 3-2 at neighbours Orient, with Billy Bonds playing with a bandage around his head to protect a gash caused by Alvin Martin's boot, then beat Swansea 2-0 at home. A tense quarter-final against Aston Villa is decided by an inexplicable handball from Villa's Ken McNaught in the last minute and a coolly taken penalty from Ray Stewart. Then Frank falls over in the semi-final replay and West Ham are at Wembley.

Cup Final day arrives with Billy Bonds cleared to play after a FA hearing ruled that he need only serve a one-match suspension for being sent off against Birmingham. Maggie Thatcher is Prime Minister, *The Empire Strikes Back* is the top-grossing film in the UK and Tom Baker is still starring in *Doctor Who*.

Dexys Midnight Runners are number one with *Geno*, having managed to fend off the Cockney Rejects' heroically aggressive version of *I'm Forever Blowing Bubbles*, which reaches number 35. The Rejects appear on *Top of the Pops* after the final on May 22 performing in West Ham shirts. The B-side to *Bubbles*, *West Side Boys*, isn't quite in the traditional Cup Final singsong tradition, with lyrics of: "Doctor Martens and iron bars! Smash the coaches and do 'em in their cars!"

FLYING SO HIGH: WEST HAM'S CUP FINALS

Wembley's match day programme features a full-page picture of The Duchess and Duke of Kent on page three. The advertising profile for a football fan appears to be based on John Thaw and Denis Waterman's characters of Regan and Carter in *The Sweeney*. It has an advert for Player's No 6 on the back cover, and inside adverts for Embassy No 1, Littlewoods Pools, Zetters Treble Chance, Skol lager ("when you know lager you're a Skolar"), Victor aftershave, Power soccer boots and Kevin Keegan's new column in the *Sunday Mirror*. We find an early attempt at merchandising as Wembley advertises branded keyrings, wristbands, sweaters, executive jotters and programme binders.

In the pen-pics of the teams there's a full-page picture of "The 'Wall' the Hammers built", a close-up shot of Stuart Pearson, Pat Holland, Paul Allen and Alan Devonshire holding their meat and two veg as they prepare to face a free kick.

The Final is on a day of hot sunshine. It's the second FA Cup Final that I've attended in five years, but not without some difficulty. My final exams at the University of Lancaster are set to begin the following Tuesday.

But football is more important than 2:1 degrees and I make my way to London in an Arsenal-supporting fellow student's car, and all without a ticket but with the rest of my term's grant in my pocket. A fan with his son outside the stadium takes pity on me and says he'll try to sneak his son under the turnstile and give me his ticket. This illicit trick works beautifully and he only charges me a fiver for a £3.50 ticket. Then it's up to the terraces and the beautiful sunlight on green turf. Wem-ber-ley!

The Irons fans are at the 'lucky end' above the tunnel. Eighties fashions on view include claret and blue rugby shirts, Admiral replica West Ham shirts with that 'V' shaped band on the chest, white West Ham scarves with claret and blue banding, and claret and white peaked caps. Plus some retro moustaches and beards from Hammers fans untouched by the spirit of punk. There won't be any repeat of the pitch invasion of 1975 though as ugly wire fences surround the pitch.

For the first time at a West Ham final, we see fans waving club flags that have been commercially made and sold on Wembley Way. But there are still plenty of home made banners too, reading: "Hitchcock's Dead but Psycho Plays On", "Get your camera off our banner", "Trevor Brooking Sells More Dummies than Mothercare", and the more poetic, "The Greatest Players in the Land are Captain Billy and his Band. That's Frank the Lamp, Alan Dev, Paul and Stewart and Tricky Trev."

The supporters have particular fun with the names Alan Devonshire and Pat Rice of Arsenal. Variations on these themes include: "Devonshire is the cream, Rice is the pudding", "Billy Bonds eats Rice", and "Devonshire is a Delight."

The advertising hoardings have the perennial Rizla ads, plus names like Talbot, Hotpoint, Mornflake Oats and DAF Trucks. Other adverts betray the 1980s' obsession with sound and vision: Pye Radio, Bush Colour TV, Hitachi, Philips, and Sharp almost have me reaching for my graphic equalizer, while several ads such as National Girobank and "Join the Union TGWU" help convey the spirit of the Thatcher years.

The Combined Bands of the Guards Division are still providing the pre-match entertainment followed by an "FA Super Skills demonstration" and *Abide With Me*.

The BBC's Bob Wilson is on the pitch doing pre-match interviews before a raucous Hammers end. When he interviews Liam Brady there's a very audible chorus of "Who the f••king hell are you?" The West Ham players are wearing light camel blazers and brown trousers.

Paul Allen is set to be the youngest player ever to appear in an FA Cup Final at the age of 17 years and 256 days. He tells Bob Wilson in his squeaky cockney accent that, "It's magic to see all the supporters an' that, I'm just going to go out there and enjoy it… it's brilliant." He's had a telegram from Howard Kendall from Preston's 1964 side wishing him luck and congratulating him on breaking his record.

David Cross mentions all the solid pros he's known like John Wile who have never played in a Wembley final. Stuart Pearson wears shades and says his neck injury is fine now. Trevor Brooking is assured and urbane, asking Bob how he is and then saying that he thinks this is a stronger Hammers line-up than in 1975. He sounds like a pundit already.

West Ham fans reading the *Daily Express* have already been incensed by comments from Brian Clough. He's said, not that unreasonably, that it is a disgrace West Ham are concentrating on the cup when they've finished seventh in Division Two and should have put all their efforts into winning promotion.

Old Big Head then comments: "Trevor Brooking floats like a butterfly... and stings like one. I have never had a high opinion of him as a player. He has been lucky enough to become a member of teams he shouldn't really have had a sniff at. I believe his lack of application and other players like him has meant relegation for West Ham in the past and the failure to win promotion this time."

It's a cheap jibe from Clough and as Brooking later said, it's odd coming from someone who once tried to buy him. Brooking refuses to comment on the day, but inside is quietly determined to prove Clough wrong. Seven years later, Clough saw Brooking in the tunnel at a Crystal Palace versus Nottingham Forest cup-tie and said to him: "Young man, a few years ago I said something before an FA Cup Final which I shouldn't have done. I'm sorry and I apologise."

Meanwhile Billy Bonds and Alvin Martin are also riled by a Friday night TV preview they've watched in the team hotel in which Alan Mullery claims that the West Ham duo don't compare to Willie Young and David O'Leary.

John Lyall leads his men on to the pitch in a brown lounge jacket and black slacks, looking like a dapper car salesman from the Eastern Avenue. The West Ham players wear claret and blue tracksuit tops. The players look fairly relaxed and even young Paul Allen, just 17 years and 256 days old, appears relatively calm. Terry Neill's Arsenal are in their yellow away kit with blue flared collars.

Bizarrely referee George Courtney and his linesmen have huge flapping white collars on their black referees' shirts. The Duchess of Kent looks regal in a purple twin-set and hat as she is introduced to the teams, while the rival fans sing *Bubbles* and "There's only one Liam Brady!"

On the BBC commentary John Motson gives us some amateur sociology about West Ham providing hope for the deprived tower blocks of the East End.

Not too much happens in the early minutes, though it's evident John Lyall has made tactical changes to the Hammers' side. Stuart Pearson is playing wide on the left and Geoff Pike and Paul Allen are wide on the right, leaving David Cross all alone up front.

It might not be traditional West Ham free-flowing attacking football, but it leaves the Arsenal defence overmanned and helps the Irons smother the influential Liam Brady in midfield.

A chorus of "We all follow the West Ham over land and sea!" echoes around the stadium while the Gooners resort to "Good old Arsenal we're proud to say your name!", a song written by Jimmy Hill, which says everything you need to know.

An early optimistic sign is a good run and cross from Pearson on the left that allows Pike to get in a snap-shot, well-saved by Pat Jennings. After 13 minutes comes the game's pivotal moment. Brooking finds Pearson, who plays the ball across the face of the Arsenal defence to Devonshire on the left. Devo takes on Rice and leaves the Arsenal man floundering, sending over a lofted cross that Jennings can only parry. The ball falls to Cross, who shoots against a defender's legs and then Pearson who miscues, firing it across the goal and Trevor Brooking shows great reflexes to divert the ball over the line with a stooping header.

My memory is of the West Ham end going mental, but no one knowing who scored until Trev's name went up on Wembley's giant scoreboard. Brian Moore didn't know either on ITV, as he initially credited the goal to Pearson. "Trevor Brooking the idol of the East End gives West Ham the lead," summarises John Motson.

John Lyall sits on the bench smoking a fag, something gaffers can't do nowadays. It really is a bench too, the sort you might find in a school assembly hall, with Lyall next to tracksuited Rob Jenkins and Terry Neill and Don Howe squashed up at the other end.

"One-nil! One-Nil!" chant the West Ham fans to the tune of *Amazing Grace*, followed by, "We're on the march with Lyall's army! We've all going to Wem-ber-ley! And we'll really shake 'em up when we win the FA Cup! 'Cos West Ham is the greatest football team!" The Gooners respond with, "You only sing when you're winning!"

West Ham hardly look like a Second Division side. What's intriguing is how easily they contain Arsenal for most of the game, played at a slow pace under a hot sun. Alvin Martin and Billy Bonds are both making vital interceptions at the back, while Trevor Brooking has a brilliant game, tackling back in defence and always available to set up an attack with a feint or a body swerve that sends an Arsenal man the wrong way before spraying a pass out wide. Young Paul Allen is shadowing Brady well and even Alan Devonshire is tackling hard in midfield.

Arsenal appear to be suffering from fatigue in their 67th match of the season, though there's little excuse for their poor delivery. Willie Young balloons a cross straight at Phil Parkes and then a corner is played straight into Parkes' hands. The big keeper is so confident that he appears to be playing the match while wearing a pair of driving gloves, the sort of thing he might use for motoring through Hornchurch on a Sunday afternoon.

It's not until half an hour has gone that Arsenal create a decent chance, Graham Rix having an effort saved by Parkes.

The West Ham fans produce a loud version of: "He's only a poor little Gunner/His face is all tattered and torn/he made me feel sick/so I hit him with a brick/and now he don't sing anymore!" Fandom has come a long way since the rattles, jackets, ties and sportsmanship of the 1964 Cup Final.

There's a worrying couple of minutes when Devonshire goes down and Paul Brush warms up, but the wiry midfielder carries on. John Motson shows off his inside knowledge to TV viewers by revealing that Devonshire is one of those players who wears padding on his ankles in addition to shinpads.

Brooking gets back to expertly tackle Willie Young on the break and after 40 minutes you know things are going well as Billy Bonds rolls his socks down and plays on without shinpads. Anybody that hard must surely intimidate the Gunners.

West Ham nearly score again on the break. Brooking plays a one-two with Pike, whose cross is nodded back by Pearson towards Devonshire. The midfielder's volley is blocked by a perfect intervention from Talbot.

"Brady is a wanker!" comes the riposte from the Irons fans after the Irishman takes issue with a Billy Bonds foul.

The half-time whistle blows and the lads head down the tunnel accompanied by flag-waving cries of "Lyall… Lyall…" followed by, "and now you're gonna believe us, we're gonna win the cup!"

Arsenal begin the second half in more determined fashion. After 52 minutes Graham Rix cuts inside Ray Stewart to send a vicious curling shot towards West Ham goal, but Parkes reacts quickly to get down and tip it away for a corner. Alvin Martin clashes heads with Willie Young while preventing an Arsenal chance. Billy Bonds still finds the energy to race down the left wing and win a corner.

Arsenal have another good chance when West Ham concede a free-kick on the edge of the box. Parkes does well to hold on to Brian Talbot's low shot. But West Ham are still looking dangerous on the counter attack, with Brooking always an outlet. It's a measure of young Paul Allen's confidence that he tries to chip the experienced Pat Jennings.

One nice thing about watching the BBC recording of the final again is to hear Jimmy Hill making a fool of himself with 20 minutes to go. Alvin Martin has had a great game but Arsenal have dominated the second half he says, and "in the end a goal will be inevitable."

The West Ham fans are starting to find some belief, and singing *Bubbles*, *You'll Never Walk Alone* and *We Shall Not Be Moved*. It's a bit like Muhammad Ali's rope-a-dope tactics against George Foreman in the 'Rumble in the Jungle' in 1974. Arsenal, still to play in the Cup Winners' Cup Final five days later, have punched themselves out.

"He's only a poor little Gunner…" wafts from the tunnel end. Ray Stewart makes a couple of good challenges and wins a vital header. Liam Brady makes a great run from the half way line but is tackled on the edge of the box by Brooking, stinging like a bee. Brian Clough's ill-chosen words inspire Trev, in his 500th West Ham appearance, to give one of his greatest performances.

Billy Bonds is getting fitter as the games goes on and makes another surging run down the left wing. His cross results in Pat Jennings making a good block from Ray Stewart, only for the move to be ruled offside.

With three minutes to go the West Ham fans are frantically whistling. Then comes the moment when the Irons will surely get the second goal to seal the game. Brooking plays a one-two with Devonshire gets the return and plays the ball inside to Paul Allen. The youngster cuts inside an Arsenal defender and has a clear run on goal. He looks certain to score in front of the West Ham legions, until Willie Young hacks him down from behind with a lunge that would be a straight red card today. "Oh what a pity!" says Motty on the BBC commentary, "a cynical foul and fully deserving of the yellow card it got."

Ray Stewart's free-kick is deflected off the wall and Arsenal and Young escape punishment. But at least some time has been used up. West Ham even have time to set up another elegant passing movement culminating in a wide cross from Pearson. The ball is with a tired-looking Graham Rix in midfield, he hoofs the ball towards the West Ham box… and the whistle blows!

An exhausted David Cross collapses on the ground with his head in his hands. Paul Allen has his head buried in the turf too. John Lyall hugs Rob Jenkins on the bench. Trevor Brooking gives Paul a fatherly hug.

Squad players Bobby Ferguson, Jimmy Neighbour and Pat Holland are on the pitch too, John Lyall has a lovely smile and embraces his senior men, Billy Bonds, Trevor Brooking and Frank Lampard. Youths in claret and blue rugby shirts punch the air and a myriad flags sway up and down at the tunnel end.

And now the players are going up the steps to the royal box. Billy Bonds' hair is ruffled by numerous hands. He's followed by Frank Lampard, Ray Stewart and Geoff Pike in a white West Ham scarf. He gives the Duchess of Kent a bone-crushing handshake and lifts the cup above his head to a thunderous roar. The players all shake the hands of Mr Len Cearns the chairman who is next to the Duchess. And then comes Paul Allen, blubbing like a kid who's had his Chopper nicked. This was ten years before Gazza made crying at football fashionable.

On ITV Brian Moore comes over all paternal: "Paul Allen is crying his eyes out, his chairman looks concerned, to think that when West Ham won the Cup in 1975 he was in the second year at comprehensive school. There he is a day and moment he'll never forget and he needn't worry about the tears today."

When you see the emotional bond that day between Allen and the club, it's sad reflecting how a few years later he was allowed to join Tottenham.

On the lap of honour a jogging Paul Allen and Geoff Pike are wearing claret and white caps and holding the Cup aloft, while Ray Stewart has the lid. The players stop for a team photo, with Alan Devonshire holding a West Ham teddy bear and the lid of the cup on Phil Parkes' head.

"One team in London! There's only one team in London!" chant the Hammers fans, adding to Arsenal's misery.

John Lyall slips away from the celebrations and stands in front of the tunnel. The cameras linger on him for half a minute just looking at the joy of the fans, thinking about the hope he's given to decent, ordinary people. My late mother, watching at home, remarked what a nice man Lyall seemed to be. This was a time when football teams and their communities were much closer. And that moment gazing at the crowd is a perfect epitaph for Lyall.

In the dressing room the normally teetotal Trevor Brooking is so carried away that he has a sip of champagne. David Cross asks if anyone has seen his legs, referring to his exhausting running. The players return to their banquet at the Grosvenor House hotel, some later celebrating at Quaglino's restaurant though they don't celebrate quite as hard as some of the staff.

Billy Bonds told the BBC: "Do I remember much about the celebrations? No, not really, apart from that I had to put our coach Ernie Gregory and physio Rob Jenkins to bed early because they had both drunk too much out of the Cup."

John Lyall recalled the usually sober Ernie Gregory singing songs from the Boer War that he'd learned in the army, all merged with *Bubbles*. Brooking moves on to a meal with friends, where a Sunderland fan sent over champagne unsuccessfully hoping that Trevor would over-celebrate before the Hammers' game at Roker Park.

My own celebrations take me to the Boleyn pub near the West Ham ground. Every car on Green Street is sounding their horn and inside the pub an Arsenal scarf is lit with a cigarette lighter and ceremonially burned in the centre of the front bar, a gesture that might not pass health and safety checks today.

On the Sunday the players take an open top bus from Stratford Broadway to East Ham Town Hall. It's less an open-top bus and more a CIS Insurance-branded coach with the sun-roof open, but somehow the players poke their torsos through. Some 200,000 Hammers fans line the route. Jugs of beer are being sent from the pubs and passed up to the players. David Cross wields a giant hammer and Geoff Pike is wearing a Hammers bobble hat and David Cross in a claret and blue cap.

Trevor Brooking remembers, "people had come out from hospitals so you could see various patients and babies being held up and crying their eyes out."

In *Just Like My Dreams,* John Lyall recalled the owner of a dodgy massage parlour leaning out of an upstairs window, standing alongside two scantily-clad masseurs, and shouting "Tell the boys John any time they want to come along – and it won't cost them a penny!"

Club photographer Steve Bacon's photos capture the mayhem outside the Boleyn pub with its Ind Coope branding and fans leaning out of the upstairs windows.

The BBC footage at East Ham town hall shows Mayoress Marjorie Helps forgetting decorum and hugging Phil Parkes and John Lyall. The fan with claret and blur hair captured by the cameras emailed the BBC 30 years later. "I had that done at a hairdressers in St Albans on the Friday morning and the local press came to take pics. It took six months to wash/grow out... Happy days!"

On East Ham town hall balcony Paul Allen is the first player to emerge, wearing a knotted claret and blue scarf around his neck. Ray Stewart is in a scarf and cap, a fresh-faced Alvin Martin next to him. "There's only one Trevor Brooking!" chant the delirious fans as Trev holds the cup while wearing a jacket and tie, unlike the open-collared colleagues.

Even the Monday *Guardian* devotes a news feature to West Ham's homecoming in the East End, headlined "Cheers from Bow to Bethnal Green" and including a picture of Paul Allen with the Cup being kissed by his mother. Among the 200,000 crowd is a policeman with a West Ham sticker on his helmet and "scarcely a dog from Bow to Bethnal Green without a rosette on its collar."

Seeing the crowds Pat Holland jokes to the *Guardian's* reporter, "We thought we'd won the war!" On the *Guardian's* sports pages there's a picture of Brooking, Bonds and Martin embracing and David Lacey cites this trio as the reason for West Ham's victory.

"How Brain And Heart Beat Destiny" is the headline in Monday's *Daily Mirror*, with Frank McGhee writing: "If Brooking was the brains of the team Bonds was the heart and few men who have ever treasured Cup winners' medals are entitled to wear them with more pride than the one which now adorns Billy's big chest."

That day's *Mirror* also has an article by Alf Garnett from the sitcom *Till Death Us Do Part*, penned by creator Johnny Speight, lambasting Brian Clough's "norf an' sarf" and throwing in some racist terms in the name of humour that would never get into a paper today.

On the back page a column by John Lyall says that the team won the final in a similar fashion to the way Hurricane Higgins played snooker, with a sense of adventure: "There's an adage I'll always go along with: 'To be successful you have to take chances.' The soccer fans wants to be excited by

men like Trevor Brooking and Alan Devonshire…
I'm just delighted for those wonderful fans of ours.
We gave them the opportunity for a typical East
London knees-up."

It's been a typically eccentric West Ham
triumph. In league terms the season has been a
failure. Anyone watching the final would wonder
why West Ham were not a top side in the Premier
League.

Two days after the final West Ham play the
final fixture of the Division Two season, away at
Sunderland. They lose 2-0, a result that guarantees
Sunderland promotion and ensures that West Ham
finish seventh, six points off the top three. The Irons
have lost twice to Shrewsbury, 3-0 away and 3-1 at
home. After reaching the final they immediately lost
home games to Birmingham and Shrewsbury yet
are now the FA Cup holders.

Today John Lyall might have been sacked for
such underachievement, and Brooking, Devonshire,
Bonds and Martin would surely have left for top-
class football rather than play another season in
Division Two.

Yet in 1980, all those players stay and the
board's patience is rewarded. Buoyed by that FA
Cup win West Ham go on to win the Division Two
championship and reach the League Cup Final the
following season, as well as playing in the Cup
Winners' Cup. Logic and West Ham have never
been easy bedfellows.

Would an earlier promotion be traded for that
epic win at Wembley? Not by most West Ham fans.
Arsenal have been humbled and proof has been

provided that Trevor Brooking can both float and sting. There is indeed only one team in London.

7. AND CLEMENCE IS DOWN ON HIS KNEES AS THEY GO TO CONGRATULATE RAY STEWART...

1981 LEAGUE CUP FINAL

LIVERPOOL 1 WEST HAM 1

Wembley Stadium, Saturday 14 March, 1981. Kick-off 3pm.

LIVERPOOL 2 WEST HAM 1

Villa Park, Wednesday, April 1 1981. Kick-off 7.30pm

WEST HAM: Phil Parkes; Ray Stewart, Alvin Martin, Billy Bonds, Frank Lampard; Jimmy Neighbour, Geoff Pike, Trevor Brooking, Alan Devonshire; David Cross, Paul Goddard. Substitute: Stuart Pearson

IF THE KITS ARE UNITED: All white Admiral kit for the Wembley match. For the replay claret shirts with two claret stripes on blue arms, white shorts with claret side stripes and white socks with claret hoops.

FACIAL HAIR: Alan Devonshire, David Cross and Phil Parkes all sport 1980s porn star moustaches. Frank Lampard still has a full beard but Billy Bonds is clean-shaven.

FLYING SO HIGH: WEST HAM'S CUP FINALS

BLOW DRY FACTOR: Phil Parkes looks to be the best user of a hairdryer, but honourable mentions to Alan Devonshire and Jimmy Neighbour.

FAN FACTOR: Flags, banners, white scarves trimmed with claret and blue, Harringtons, straight jeans.

ATTENDANCE: 100,000 at Wembley, 36,693 for the replay.

PRICE OF PROGRAMME: 60p at Wembley, 50p at Villa Park.

It seems like West Ham are going to be at Wembley every year. The Irons are top of Division Two and heading towards the title. They've also found time to compete in the Cup Winners' Cup and get to the League Cup Final. The Hammers have beaten Burnley, Charlton and Barnsley in the early stages.

David Cross scored the winner against Spurs in the quarter-final at a packed Upton Park. West Ham lost 3-2 away to Coventry in the first leg of the semi final, after being 2-0 up. Had they blown it? In the return leg at Upton Park a fantastic turn and strike from Paul Goddard put the Hammers level on aggregate before Jimmy Neighbour, newly signed from Norwich, scored the winner and took the Hammers back to Wembley just ten months after beating Arsenal in the FA Cup Final.

On Cup Final morning a group of us are donning black Harringtons, Levi's jeans and claret and blue scarves to head from Brentwood to Wem-ber-ley. We've had to queue on a Sunday morning at Upton Park for tickets. Some fans had queued overnight and the club programme *Hammer* lamented: "The blaring of transistor radios, use of front gardens as toilets, theft of milk and abuse of those who protested is not conducive to good public relations between our neighbours and ourselves."

Once again *I'm Forever Blowing Bubbles* rings out at Wembley as John Lyall leads out the Hammers. Neighbour replaces the injured Paul Allen from the FA Cup-winning team and the big signing from QPR, Paul Goddard is in for Stuart Pearson, who is now on the bench.

The hoardings denote the giant companies of the early 1980s, with names like Pioneer, Canon, Hitachi and Toyota alongside Electrolux, Midland Bank, Daily Mirror, Norwich Union, Just Juice and Flash Plug. *Jealous Guy*, Roxy Music's tribute to John Lennon, is number one. That Saturday Tom Baker is appearing in his final *Doctor Who* story *Logopolis.*

The Wembley programme has adverts for Embassy cigarettes, Skol lager, Curries Motors, Power football boots, Littlewoods and Zetters Pools, Canon cameras, Robinson Willey gas fires, and the film *Loophole* starring Albert Finney and Martin Sheen. On a specifically West Ham theme we have Trevor Brooking posing in Dunlop Superstars boots and an offer of "maroon/sky" West Ham footballs for £12.

The game is tight and both sides create chances. Bonds heads over from Brooking's free kick, but is ruled offside. Liverpool think they've scored when a free kick is played to Sammy Lee who scores with a fine shot into the corner, only for Irwin to be correctly ruled offside.

Phil Parkes makes a superb one-handed save from Dalglish's header. Frank Lampard shoots low and just wide of post. Parkes then saves with his feet from Neal's low cross-come shot.

On the half-way line Trevor Brooking plays through Paul Goddard only for the West Ham man to hastily lob over bar. Bonds heads wide from Brooking's free kick and then it's into extra-time. The second division side have matched Liverpool for 90 minutes.

Extra time sees Neighbour cross and Devonshire head wide, while Jimmy Case thumps the top of Phil Parkes' crossbar. Ray Kennedy pokes wide for the 'Pool. A David Cross header from a Lampard flick produces a great save from Clemence, but is ruled offside.

Bizarrely most of the action is in the last three minutes of extra time. *Bubbles* is echoing around Wembley as Liverpool win a free kick on the edge of the box. Jimmy Case's shot is blocked. The ball is returned into the mixer, Irwin chips it into the box, Billy Bonds gets his head to the ball and Alvin Martin hacks a hasty clearance away from the six-yard line. The ball falls to Alan Kennedy on the edge of the area. His right-foot shot passes a few inches above the prostrate — and offside —Sammy Lee and fizzes into the net. Referee Clive Thomas points to the centre circle.

"No, it's not going to count! Is it going to count? They're going over to the linesman... Yes, it is going to count!" says an excitable Barry Davies on the BBC commentary.

The West Ham players rush over to remonstrate with the linesman who appears to have flagged Lee offside, led by Stuart Pearson, followed by Geoff Pike, David 'Psycho' Cross, Alan Devonshire and Ray Stewart. Even Trevor Booking joins in.

Thomas comes over to discuss matters with the Lino and after a brief discussion, he points to the centre spot and runs away in the fashion of a pedantic games master. Lee was not interfering with play says the ref.

Alan Devonshire waves his arms in frustration and probably uses some industrial language, while even the phlegmatic Trevor Brooking appears to be uttering something like "Dash it, man!"

Most teams would have given up at this point as the Liverpool fans wave their scarves and begin a massed victory anthem of *You'll Never Walk Alone*. But the West Ham side of 1981 makes one last charge upfield. Jimmy Neighbour gets a cross into the box and Alan Devonshire is clattered by Alan Hansen on the edge of the area. Ray 'Tonka' Stewart produces a thunderous free kick that is tipped round the post by a sprawling Ray Clemence. Great save.

So it's one last corner. Jimmy Neighbour swings it in and Alvin Martin rises above two defenders to power a header towards the top corner of the net. Terry McDermott is on the post and palms the ball on to the crossbar. Penalty! Alvin Martin punches the air.

Today McDermott would have been sent off, but the Liverpool man with the Harry Enfield Scouser perm and 'tache is left unpunished. So it's all down to Ray Stewart with what must be the last kick of the game.

Ray looks nerveless as he picks up the ball. But instead of using his usual technique of blasting ball and goalkeeper through the back of the net, Stewart calmly slots the ball along the ground and into the right hand side of the net as Clemence dives the wrong way. "And he puts it in! And Clemence is down on his knees as they go to congratulate Ray Stewart," enthuses Barry Davies on the BBC commentary.

The West Ham fans behind the goal erupt with joy and relief. Stewart raises both arms and is mobbed by Pike and Cross. We've matched the best team in the country and maybe Europe. The whistle blows and a replay beckons at Villa Park.

John Lyall dashes on to the pitch in his black raincoat to pat Ray Stewart on the back and clench a gloved fist in triumph, reminding me a little of Alvin Stardust.

He then walks over to Clive Thomas and tells him, "We feel cheated." Honest John Lyall is reported to the FA by Thomas, who believes that the West Ham boss has accused him of cheating. After some "Big bad John" headlines, Lyall calls youth coach Tony Carr as a witness and is exonerated by the FA hearing. In typical style, he has lunch with Thomas afterwards and they leave "the best of friends."

W est Ham are back in claret and blue shirts for the replay, with Liverpool changing to white shirts and black shorts. Controversially, ITV is screening the match live, which has affected the attendance of 36,693.

The Hammers start almost too well. Nine minutes in Trevor Brooking shimmies and finds Jimmy Neighbour on the half-way line. The former Tottenham man produces a glorious old-fashioned winger's run. The West Ham fans in the Holt End offer a collective roar of encouragement as Jimmy races towards the far end. He shows Alan Hansen the ball, but then whips it past his clumsy challenge, making the future pundit look guilty of diabolical defending. Neighbour sprints to the byline and crosses to the near-post, where Paul Goddard scores with a fantastic diving header.

"And he's gone past Alan Hansen… he's got a couple of West Ham players waiting in the middle… Ah… and it's there!" hollers Brian Moore on the ITV commentary. "One-nil… one-nil!" chant the West Ham fans followed by, "We're gonna win the Cup!" and *Bubbles*.

West Ham's early goal sparks Liverpool into showing all their class. A long-range effort from Sammy Lee forces Parkes to make a good save. Some 19-year-old kid called Ian Rush is making his second full appearance for Liverpool and hits the angle of post and bar after latching on to a swiftly-taken free kick. Then Ray Kennedy hits the crossbar with a header from a corner. Like David Bowie and Queen we're *Under Pressure*.

After 25 minutes McDermott chips a ball over the West Ham defence and as the ball dips over his shoulder Kenny Dalglish scores with a brilliant diagonal volley. Liverpool mount even more pressure and three minutes later they win a corner. Case takes it and Hansen climbs to get in a powerful header that deflects off Billy Bonds' outstretched thigh and into the net past Phil Parkes' despairing dive. It's tough on the heroic Bonzo.

The Irons could have folded at this point. But West Ham dominate much of the second half, with Brooking, Devonshire and the underrated Pike playing well in midfield and Neighbour threatening on the right. Alvin Martin shoots into Clemence's midriff from a corner and then a Liverpool free kick sees Parkes catch Neal's effort. The West Ham custodian tips Dalglish's shot past the post. After that West Ham have a lot of possession and get in several dangerous crosses. "West Ham haven't wilted," declares Brian Clough on the live ITV commentary.

With 15 minutes left Pike plays in Brooking who almost levels when he wriggles between two defenders in the box and curls the ball just wide of the post. Trev should probably have scored. "Goalscorers hit the target," declares Clough. Liverpool respond with Rush flashing the ball across the West Ham goal and Dalglish getting a good shot in on the turn.

At the end West Ham look the fitter side. "Come on you Irons!" chants the Holt End. Two minutes from time Brooking takes a free kick and Bonds sends a free header over the bar. "My how

100

they've battled, West Ham," says Brian Moore. With half a minute left Neighbour hassles Jimmy Case in the box and the ball falls to David Cross on the six-yard line. Psycho pulls a shot across Clemence and sees it roll agonisingly across the line and past the far post.

The whistle blows. Liverpool lift the League Cup for the first time. "West Ham come out of it with a good deal of honour," declares Brian Moore. Phil Parkes is interviewed on the pitch and says of his great saves. "That's what I'm paid for, but I really enjoyed it, it was a fantastic atmosphere. There was a couple of chances at the end where we could have just sneaked an equaliser."

Billy Bonds, clean-shaven and wearing a medallion, leads the losing side up first to receive their medals. Jimmy Neighbour is wearing a West Ham scarf, the experienced Stuart Pearson manages a smile and Trevor Brooking looks rueful. "WELL PLAYED WEST HAM," reads the electronic scoreboard.

Liverpool then step up to the stand to receive the Cup and hordes of young Scousers run on the pitch to mob Ray Clemence as he runs towards the stand with the trophy.

On a personal level the end of the final sees the nastier side of 1980s football. My West Ham crew of Steve, Snivs, Dayo and myself drive to Coventry to stay with our friend Alison, who is a student at Warwick University. We stop in a seemingly deserted chip shop in Hillfields. Suddenly a group of Coventry fans run out of a nearby pub and start attacking us, having seen our scarves.

"Are you the lot that got us last time?" one of them asks. No, we're not the ICF, actually. It all goes into slow motion and I feel a punch across the back and a kick round the ankles. No point in fighting back as there's too many of them.

Someone runs over the roof of the car, someone else tries to punch Steve in the car. Another Coventry hooligan smashes a bottle on a wall and slashes Snivs' arm. The miscreants see blood and perhaps this scares them off as we manage to get in the car and speed off, shaken but fairly intact. The broken bottle has missed Snivs' veins, fortunately.

It all seems incredibly stupid after watching a great game. Football is better than this. We survive, but it is to take the tragedies of Bradford, Heysel and Hillsborough, the Taylor Report and the advent of fanzines and spectator power before the game reinvents itself as a more peaceful pastime.

The next day the papers say nice things about West Ham and we're all proud of our side for the way we've performed against the great Liverpool side. Promotion is won three days later against Bristol Rovers at Upton Park, followed by the Second Division Championship with a 5-1 thrashing of Grimsby. West Ham look to be on the verge of a great era and will surely be back at Wembley within 31 years. Won't we?

8. HE CAME FROM WHITE HART LANE HE'S BETTER THAN JERMAIN... ZAMORA!

2005 CHAMPIONSHIP PLAY-OFF FINAL

WEST HAM UNITED 1 PRESTON NORTH END 0

Millennium Stadium, Cardiff. Monday May 30, 2005. Kick-off 3pm.

WEST HAM: Jimmy Walker (Stephen Bywater 87); Tomas Repka, Anton Ferdinand, Elliott Ward, Chris Powell; Shaun Newton (Mark Noble 82), Hayden Mullins, Nigel Reo-Coker, Matthew Etherington; Marlon Harewood, Bobby Zamora (Christian Dailly 74). Subs not used: Teddy Sheringham, Carl Fletcher.

IF THE KITS ARE UNITED: Claret and blue Reebok shirts with white flash on collar and Jobserve logo, white shorts and light blue socks. An orange goalkeeper's shirt for Jimmy Walker.

FACIAL HAIR: Light beard from Jimmy Walker, cool goatee from Anton Ferdinand, Czech assassin's stubbly goatee from Tomas Repka.

BLOW DRY FACTOR: Elliott Ward looks like the love child of Billy Bonds and Chewbacca with his hairy mane; it's convict crops for Bobby Zamora and Stephen Bywater, braids from Anton Ferdinand, and a

FLYING SO HIGH: WEST HAM'S CUP FINALS

cameo from Christian "I want curly hair too!" Dailly.

FAN FACTOR: Chequered claret and blue flags, naked torsos, St George's Cross flags with Basildon and Paddock Wood written on them, Paolo Di Canio's head on a stick, Cockney Rejects t-shirts.

ATTENDANCE: 70,275

PRICE OF PROGRAMME: £5

Alan Pardew's claret and blue army are returning to the Millennium Stadium — Wembley is being rebuilt — having lost the previous year's Championship Play-Off final to Crystal Palace. The Irons have spent two long years in the Championship and sold half the England side in Rio Ferdinand, Frank Lampard, Joe Cole, Jermain Defoe, Michael Carrick and Glen Johnson.

The Premier League parachute payments are running out and it's quite possible that the side will be marooned in the lower divisions for the next decade if they don't win this match. The rumour is that Pardew will be sacked if they fail. They are now relying on bargain signings like Shaun "he only cost ten grand" Newton. Yet there's also the tantalising hope of promotion and a £30 million boost to the club's budget. It's the most important match in football.

In May 2005 Tony Blair is Prime Minister, Oasis have hit the number one spot with *Lyla* and Christopher Eccleston is starring in the newly-returned *Doctor Who*. But the real issue is can West Ham get back to the Premier League.

The Hammers have only scraped into the Play-Offs, finishing sixth in the Championship. It looks like they're going to miss out on the final when the side lose a two-goal lead at home to Ipswich in the semi-final. But in the second leg, inspired by loyal choruses of "We all follow the West Ham over land and sea!", two goals from Bobby Zamora see the Hammers win at Portman Road in a confidence-boosting performance.

As ever there's a huge turnout of supporters travelling down the M4, including stretch-limos and even a fire engine full of West Ham fans. I'm travelling with my pals Nigel and Fraser having stayed overnight at Nigel's Kew Gardens home, though sadly he's forgotten his "Kew Gardens Irons" flag. We meet fellow fans Matt and Lisa in the cacophonous streets around Cardiff. "We've got Paolo Di Canio's on a stick!" chant the fans with paper heads on sticks outside the numerous pubs.

The Millennium Stadium has three tiers and in the West Ham section banners reference Chelsea's Special One with "Look out Mourinho, Hammers 'R' coming." Other banners say, "I love Teddy", "Di Canio Forever", "Paddock Wood Irons." Then there's the lad mag influenced "Mattie Etherington lays on more balls than Abi Titmuss…"

The programme costs a fiver and has adverts for the RAF and Navy, Amundsen vodka, Nescafe, Skoda, Nobby's Crisps, Tissot Swiss watches and Siemens T65 camera phones.

Thankfully club announcer Jeremy Nicholas is allowed to play *Bubbles* before the kick-off while Preston's man plays their *Pigbag* theme. Hopefully the players will benefit from losing last season's final and they at least raise smiles and look reasonably confident as they shake hands with the dignitaries before the kick-off.

West Ham start well and hit the post after four minutes. Zamora finds Shaun Newton and Ten Grand plays in a finely-weighted ball to the overlapping Repka on the right side of the box. It's a tight angle and Tomas, a West Ham goalscoring virgin, fires against the post in his last ever game for the Hammers. At least he gets a chorus of "Super Tomas Repka!" from the fans and he has emerged as a better and more disciplined player under Pards.

After a goalless first-half West Ham step up the pressure after the break and have three efforts in one move. Nigel Reo-Coker makes a fine run and plays in Marlon Harewood, only for Carlo Nash to produce a great one-handed save. The ball rebounds to Bobby Zamora who swivels to volley at goal only for Mawene to clear off the line. The ball falls to Harewood again, but Nash makes another smothering save.

The crucial breakthrough comes on 57 minutes as the West Ham subs are warming up. Zamora finds Matthew Etherington on the left. West Ham's left winger gambles on an early cross, Claude Davis slips and Bobby Zamora produces a cushioned volley to stroke the ball home in front of the West Ham fans. Yes!

Bobby leaps into the arms of subs Mark Noble, Teddy Sheringham and Carl Fletcher. They gyrate in front of Coca Cola and "Think Road Safety" logos on the billboards, while orange-bibbed stewards try to contain an erupting mass of geezers in replica shirts. One of the West Ham fans, near a bloke with a Cockney Rejects t-shirt and medallion, is holding what today seems like a giant camera and snaps a quick picture of Bobby celebrating.

"Zamora! He's done it this time! Bobby Zamora is the man of the moment, the man of the Millennium Stadium and West Ham have the lead in the Championship Play-Off Final!" declares the commentator on Sky. Summariser Chris Kamara gets very shouty, hollering, "It's a fantastic ball from Matthew Etherington… This is easy for Bobby Zamora and he makes it look easy!"

As West Ham try to play out the game, gaffer Alan Pardew causes bemusement among the fans by taking off his goalscorer, Zamora, and replacing him with football genius Christian Dailly, playing as an extra midfielder. It's a brave if slightly negative move and Dailly does well calming down the game.

Preston's Nugent fires into Walker's arms and substitute Mark Noble goes close with an attempted chip. There's a horrible moment when, with just two minute left, goalkeeper Jimmy Walker is injured on the edge of his box and is down for several aeons. He is carried off on a stretcher and replaced by substitute keeper Stephen Bywater. As soon as he's on the pitch Bywater has to face a dangerous free-kick and every West Ham fan anticipates Preston will score. McKenna's shot is hard and low but to huge relief Bywater gets his body behind it.

More purgatory comes with the fourth official announcing that will be seven minutes of added time. Seven! Somehow the Hammers get through several eternities of added time. Preston mess up an attack, Repka takes a throw-on, Etherington is about to get the ball and suddenly he's jumping up with his arms in the air and there's an explosion of desperate relief from the claret and blue army.

The players collapse in a heap of writhing humanity and Alan Pardew is raised five feet off the ground in the melee. Then the players, subs and staff gather in a giant circular hugging formation. Goalkeeping coach Ludek Miklosko and Stephen Bywater help carry the injured Jimmy Walker on to the pitch to celebrate. His leg is swathed in white bandages.

For some reason the PA plays *Is This The Way To Amarillo?* By Peter Kay. Even though Kay's a Bolton fan it fits the celebratory mood as the Irons' legions bounce up and down to the old Tony Christie classic. Young Mark Noble has taken his shirt off and is manically waving a pair of flags in time to the music.

My main thought is that we get back our ten pages devoted to each Premier League club on ITV's Teletext. In 2005 Teletext and Ceefax are still the fans' choice for club news. And after two years we're back on *Match of the Day* with Alan Hansen lambasting our defence. In the Championship trying to find West Ham's highlights on ITV's *Soccer Sunday* or *Sky Sports News* requires more technical expertise than landing a robot space probe in a specific crater on Mars.

My phone is buzzing with messages and I text my family. My four-year-old daughter Nell asks if the goalkeeper died. Later that year I marry my partner Nicola having promised to lead her up the aisle if West Ham are promoted, England win the Ashes and *Doctor Who* returns all in the same year.

Mattie Etherington is wearing a flag sarong-style, while Christian Dailly uses his as a cape as the players receive their medals from Charlotte Oades, Coca Cola's GB President. Mark Noble has his shirt on backwards. They're standing on a red Coca Cola podium in the middle of the pitch as the fans' *I'm Forever Blowing Bubbles* resonates over Wales. And then Nigel Reo-Coker and Christian Dailly jointly hold up the trophy and the side disappears underneath a barrage of claret and blue streamers.

Champagne sprays and Elliott Ward hits teammates on the head with an inflatable hammer. It's *Bubbles* on the PA and the players are holding up their arms and singing along. Alan Pardew does a dad dance on the pitch with his two young daughters. Even reclusive chairman Terry Brown is out there giving a rare interview. Chris Powell and Mark Noble run round the pitch with West Ham scarves tied bandana-style round their heads.

Alan Pardew later sums the moment up: "Two years ago all I heard was negative stuff. We're not playing this way or playing that way, he's not good enough, I'm not good enough, the chairman's not good enough. It was a cycle of misery, but we have broken the chain."

Scarves adorn every returning car on the M4. Nigel drives back to Hammersmith and makes a gig by axeman Yngwie Malmsteen, while I celebrate with Fraser in the George pub and then enjoy a single malt whisky at home while watching the highlights on ITV.

Never mind Liverpool's feats in Istanbul the previous Wednesday. West Ham appear on the front page of the next day's *Guardian* and the report, headlined "Zamora strikes gold for Hammers", describes it as "the most valuable goal in world football." The *Sun's* headline is "Lovely Bubbly... Up the Zammers... Bobby shows bottle as he fires Pardew heroes back into the big time."

An astonishing 70,000 fans turn out for the victory parade around Upton Park, covered live on *Sky Sports News*. It wouldn't be West Ham if there wasn't a glitch though. Alan Pardew is starting to sound like an Old Testament prophet, declaring: "We've come out of the darkness and into the light of the Premiership..." Then the microphone goes dead. So the fans are left to sing *Bubbles* and salute the silent players on the balcony of the Dr Martens Stand.

It doesn't matter though. Because West Ham United are back in the Premier League and Alan Pardew's cycle of misery has finally been broken.

9. THE GREATEST CUP FINAL OF MODERN TIMES

2006 FA CUP FINAL

WEST HAM UNITED 3 LIVERPOOL 3

Millennium Stadium, Cardiff. Saturday May 13 2006. Kick-off 3pm.

WEST HAM: Shaka Hislop; Lionel Scaloni, Danny Gabbidon, Anton Ferdinand, Paul Konchesky; Yossi Benayoun, Carl Fletcher (Dailly 77), Nigel Reo-Coker, Matthew Etherington (Sheringham 85), Marlon Harewood, Dean Ashton (Zamora 71). Substitutes: Jimmy Walker, James Collins, Bobby Zamora, Christian Dailly, Teddy Sheringham.

IF THE KITS ARE UNITED: All white with navy blue trim on shirts and shorts. Plus white cycling shorts for Dean Ashton's dodgy hamstring. Claret and yellow full club crest on shirts and shorts, Jobserve logo on shirts.

FACIAL HAIR: The hint of a wispy black goatee from Yossi Benayoun. Danny Gabbidon has a Marvin Gaye-style soulful growth on his chin.

BLOW DRY FACTOR: Braids from Anton Ferdinand, shaved head from Paul Konchesky, fine curly hair from Christian Dailly.

111

FAN FACTOR: Claret and blue Afro wigs, jester hats, hammers painted on cheeks, Trevor Brooking's head on a stick, chequered flags, Cross of St George flags, 'CUP FINAL 06' on the back of replica shirts.

ATTENDANCE: 74,000.

PRICE OF PROGRAMME: £8.50

After 26 long years, West Ham are back in the FA Cup Final and facing Rafael Benitez's Liverpool. That's the Liverpool side that had won the European Champions' League in Istanbul the previous summer.

Alan Pardew's newly-promoted side has finished a commendable ninth in the Premier League and reached the FA Cup Final after an emotional victory against Middlesbrough in the semi-final at Villa Park. By a strange and sad coincidence, both Ron Greenwood and John Lyall have died that month and a minute's silence for both men is held before the kick-off.

Well, it's meant to be a minute's silence until some brave soul chants "Johnny Lyall's claret and blue army!" and then 20,000 West Ham fans follow. It's a tremendous tribute to a West Ham legend.

The semi-final is a cagey game until Marlon Harewood scores with a tremendous drive, then whips off his shirt and runs to the West Ham fans, looking close to tears. Alan Pardew does a bizarre dad dance on the touchline. Boro's Riggott misses a great chance late on and then the whistle blows and West Ham are back in the Cup Final.

It's been 26 years of hurt, a period where West Ham have sold half the England side. On the same day the previous year the Irons were drawing at Brighton in the Championship. The couple sitting behind us are sobbing at the final whistle.

Anton Ferdinand does some moves, *Bubbles* and "Johnny Lyall's claret and blue army!" resound around Villa Park and the long wait has ended. West Ham's cup run has seen them beat Norwich away, Blackburn at home, Bolton in a replay at Upton Park and Manchester City away in the earlier rounds.

Not only are West Ham back in the Cup Final, but regardless of the result in the final they will qualify for the UEFA Cup, as opponents Liverpool are already in the Champions League.

The only slight sadness is that thanks to missed deadlines in developing the new Wembley, this is the last final that will be played at the Millennium Stadium, Cardiff. The Irons are used to it though, having been to Cardiff in the two previous seasons for Play-Off finals.

In May 2006 Tony Blair is still the Prime Minister, bankers need only light-touch regulation, David Tennant is starring in *Doctor Who* and the number one single is *Crazy* by Gnarls Barkley. Football has been through huge changes since 1980. The Hillsborough stadium disaster, the Taylor Report, all-seater stadia, the Premier League, middle-class fans, gates going up instead of declining, the advent of Andy Gray and Richard

Keys on the all-powerful live Sky TV coverage and footballers now earning more in a day than most people earn in a year.

Alan Pardew's claret and blue army proceeds to Wales via trains from Paddington, cars, vans and stretch limos. The programme is a pricey £8.50 and comes with a spine. Wembley now has 'official partners' with their logos on the rolling electronic hoardings around the pitch rather than Rizla boards. The programme has adverts for Pepsi Max, Umbro, Ford Focus ST motors, Umbro.com, McDonald's and Carlsberg.

The tight streets around the stadium are packed with fans and resound to the sound of horns. The numerous pubs are overflowing with noise and supporters and there's a group of West Ham fans carrying cut-out heads on sticks of Trevor Brooking, Alan Devonshire, Geoff Pike, Paolo Di Canio and Frank McAvennie.

Where once there was terracing now the final is all-seater and my ticket costs £65. Before the kick-off huge team crests move from the stands to the centre circle where there's a giant FA Cup logo. Claret and blue and red and white streamers flutter in the air. The West Ham fans carry chequered claret and blue flags and wear claret and blue Afro wigs.

The three tiers of the stadium provide ample frontage for St George's Cross flags and banners with messages such as, "Lyall Style Pardew's Cockney Kings", "Billericay Irons" and "Maldon Hammers." Before the kick-off the PA plays *You'll Never Walk Alone* and *I'm Forever Blowing*

114

Bubbles and then it's the always-emotional *Abide With Me*.

As the match begins Liverpool misplace a number of passes and the Hammers fans sense an upset. Then something incredible happens. Poor Lionel Scaloni is seen as the villain of the final today. Yet it's commonly forgotten that Scaloni makes the first goal with a brilliant run from the halfway line after 21 minutes.

Alonso plays a loose ball — never any good at ball retention those Spaniards — and Yossi Benayoun gathers it up to play in Ashton on the edge of box. Deano makes a superbly weighted pass inside the defence to the overlapping Scaloni, who crosses hard and low. There's not much chance of it reaching Marlon Harewood as either Carragher of Reina will surely deal with it. But their indecision is final. Carragher prods out a boot to try and clear the ball for a corner only to prod it in to the corner of the net. At the other end of the Millennium Stadium the West Ham fans erupt in disbelief.

Inspired by the goal, West Ham look sharper all over the pitch. Seven minutes later a throw-in is crossed to Dean Ashton and he finds Etherington with his header. Etherington cuts inside and unleashes a hard low shot that Reina should have covered, but the ball squirms away from his body and Ashton, in the place where all good strikers should be, pokes the ball past him. It rolls slowly into the net and no-one can quite believe it.

"Ole ole ole! Deano! Deano!" and then *Bubbles* wafts from the Cockney end of Cardiff. 2-0 up after 28 minutes. What could possibly go wrong? A warning comes a couple of minutes later when Crouch is ruled narrowly offside after netting from Gerrard's quickly-taken free-kick.

Four minutes after West Ham go two-nil up Liverpool pull one back. The West Ham fans are chanting "Come on you Irons!" as Gerrard is given too much space in midfield and tries a long ball. Cisse has moved to the left and gets in behind Scaloni to volley home. It's a fine finish on the full volley. Anton Ferdinand vainly appeals for offside.

Liverpool press for the rest of the half though West Ham still look dangerous on the break with Reo-Coker a fine defensive shield, Etherington lively and Dean Ashton giving a performance reminiscent of a young Geoff Hurst. Ashton drifts across the box and cleverly gets a shot in just past the post. Then Deano's header sets up Benayoun for a weak shot at the keeper.

"We all follow the West Ham over land and sea…" heralds the end of the half. Three goals in 11 minutes, but at least West Ham are still winning.

Thirty seconds into the second half West Ham almost snatch a third. Ashton chests the ball down and finds Etherington. The West Ham winger gets in a low cross and Harewood connects only to fire the ball against Reina's feet. Benayoun gets the rebound, swerves past a defender and shoots, but Reina's foot again denies West Ham.

Will that miss prove costly? It seems so after 54 minutes. Reo-Coker gives away a cheap free kick when he holds back Riise outside the area. Gerrard crosses, Crouch heads it back towards the penalty spot. The West Ham defence is for once guilty of ball watching and Gerrard meets the ball on the half volley to blast into the top of the net, whereas most other players would have skied it over the bar. The Liverpool fans break into a chorus of "We shall not be moved!"

The influential Benayoun tries to calm it down in midfield and holds the ball up well. Ashton forces a corner and the Hammers are coming back into the game. On 64 minutes Etherington finds Konchesky wide on the left. The West Ham fullback fires in a cross that sails high over Reina's head and into the top corner.

The West Ham fans at that end leap up as one entity in delirious disbelief. Konch runs into the arms of substitutes Teddy Sheringham and Bobby Zamora before being mobbed by the rest of the side. OK, maybe it wasn't a cross. Actually it was a superb Pele-like lob, Konchesky having seen Reina slightly off his line.

"You're not singing anymore!" chant the Irons fans. What a final. Then it's: "We all follow the West Ham over land and sea..."

West Ham appear to be controlling the game now. Etherington fires a cross across the goal and Reo-Coker blazes wide of goal from the left. Zamora comes on for Ashton and receives a chorus of, "He comes from White Hart Lane, he's better than Jermain..." Christian Dailly replaces Fletcher to provide experience in midfield

Danny Gabbidon heads another cross away. On the BBC Mark Lawrenson describe him as a magnet and John Motson adds, "he's a rock". Benayoun is having a superb game. Reina slips as another dangerous Etherington cross goes across goal. *Bubbles* is sung in hope and then, "When Nige goes up to lift the FA Cup, we'll be there!"

On 87 minutes Liverpool are awarded a free kick outside the area and Steven Gerrard blazes wildly wide. The West Ham fans are jumping up and down, daring to celebrate. The Liverpool captain has received a knock and on the BBC Mark Lawrenson says, "West Ham are effectively playing ten men, because Gerrard's out of it." Yeah, right.

It's now the 89th minute and glory is so close. In West Ham's penalty area on-loan right back Lionel Scaloni sees that Liverpool's Djbril Cisse has pulled up with a muscle strain and deliberately puts the ball into touch, prompting John Motson to remark on what a sporting gesture it is. Cisse is treated and from the throw-in the ball is given back to Scaloni by Liverpool, as footballing etiquette dictates.

Rather than take a touch Scaloni volleys it, only instead of hitting it way down the field or hoofing it into touch, he slices the ball infield. It's controlled by Gerrard, who passes to Riise. The left back crosses the ball into the box. Danny Gabbidon heads it out of the area, Benayoun nudges it on and the ball falls perfectly for the loitering Steven Gerrard. No danger there then. He's injured and exhausted, so out of desperation the Liverpool maestro unleashes a 35-yard shot that will surely balloon over the bar. The PA is just announcing: "The fourth official has indicated there will be added time of four minutes."

118

But in one of those terrible slow motion moments when the very space-time continuum seems to be shaken, the ball arrows into the bottom corner of Shaka Hislop's goal with the force of a small thermonuclear missile.

It's one of the greatest goals ever seen in the FA Cup Final and ties the game up at 3-3. It's the moment where every West Ham wishes they had a Tardis and could go back in time to change history by telling Scaloni to just hoof it, even if it meant disrupting the time line, therefore meaning they had never been born.

It's not entirely Scaloni's fault, as no-one is marking Gerrard, and he's played a part in the first two goals. But sadly for him that will be forgotten and he will be forever associated with costing West Ham the FA Cup.

"Take a bow son, take a bow!" exclaims Andy Gray on the Sky TV coverage. Gerrard points to the name on the back of his shirt, as if we needed to know. From my seat in block M22 I can recall feeling a horrible sense of deflation, at the same time tinged with awareness that we were seeing football history and one of the greatest goals ever scored at Wembley. Why always West Ham?

The ball enters the net at 90 minutes and nine seconds. There's still time for Sheringham to win a free kick on the edge of the Liverpool area. Konchesky drives hard and low through the Liverpool wall but Reina is down to save smartly.

The referee signals the end of normal time and the players collapse exhausted on to the turf. Extra time is strangely muted, both players and fans appear drained by such a pulsating first 94 minutes. Liverpool have more pressure in the first half and Riise fires a long-range shot just over.

Three players are down in the 21st minute of extra time, Gerrard with cramp and Harewood and Sissoko after a clumsy tackle from the Liverpool man. "It's like a battlefield out there!" exclaims John Motson. Harewood can hardly walk and has to go off the field for a couple of minutes to have his ankle strapped. His return gets a big chorus of "There's only one Marlon 'Arewood!"

Zamora has fresh legs and makes a couple of powerful runs. With two minutes to go he's fouled on the left wing. Benayoun swings in the free kick, and the ball deflects off the back of Nigel Reo-Coker's head towards the Liverpool goal. Reina somehow tips it onto the post. The ball rebounds back across the face of the goal and falls to, of all people, the injured Marlon Harewood. He can hardly raise his foot and just can't get his leg around the ball, slicing it wide. A fit Marlon would surely have scored.

On the BBC John Motson comments: "You almost think that the gods are not smiling on West Ham… Arguably the best Cup Final of modern times is going to be settled by a shoot-out."

It all rests on Shaka, in for the injured Roy Carroll. The shoot-out is at the West Ham end. Liverpool start the shoot-out. Dietmar Hamann hesitates slightly at the penalty spot before scoring with ease, despite the desperate arm waving of the Hammers fans behind the goal.

Bobby Zamora never looks completely confident in his run-up, but his kick is in the corner, though not powerful enough. Reina pulls off a great save. Then Sami Hypia's penalty is saved low by Shaka Hislop, to great cheers from the fans behind him. The 40-year-old Teddy Sheringham scores confidently and gives a Stuart Pearce-style "Come on!" to the crowd. It's now 1-1.

Inevitably Steven Gerrard scores with his penalty to put Liverpool 2-1 up. Then it's Paul Konchesky, who so nearly scored the winning goal in a Cup Final. He puts it down the middle and Reina leaves his legs there to save. Poor Konch pulls his shirt up over his mouth and looks distraught. Riise takes a similar penalty to Konchesky, but scores through the middle.

So now if Anton Ferdinand misses Liverpool have won the cup. It's not hit with enough power and Reina dives to his left to parry the ball. Anton kicks the rebound high over the bar in frustration and falls to his knees. The Liverpool players rush to embrace Reina and the cup is theirs. Ferdinand is consoled by Roy Carroll and then the rest of the side.

Fans are in tears behind the goal, but are still full of pride at West Ham's performance. No one leaves early, instead all you can hear as Reo-Coker, Reina and Gerrard are interviewed on the pitch is a huge chorus of *I'm Forever Blowing Bubbles*.

Consoling texts arrive from all around the country. West Ham's young captain Nigel Reo-Coker leads his team to the plinth on the centre circle to collect their runners-up medals. The

Scousers generously applaud. As Gerrard then moves up to take the trophy another huge chorus of *Bubbles* graces the Millennium stadium.

My final ends with an exhausted walk by the River Taff to Llandaff where I'm staying with Cardiff-based friends, and a pint of Brains beer feeling devastated, yet also privileged to have watched the greatest of Cup Finals. At least we turned up, unlike many a previous finalist, and we so nearly won it. And at least we're still in Europe.

The press is universal in its praise for West Ham. "Everyone's a winner as old magic returns to grand finale: Showpiece at last lives up to its reputation and joins legendary finals of 1953 and '73," is the headline above Patrick Collins' verdict in the *Mail on Sunday*.

"First it was the Matthews Final – and now it's the Gerrard Final," reads The *News of the World*, "Stevie stars in best final ever."

The *News of the World's* Martin Samuel, a West Ham fan, writes: "As West Ham trooped shattered, heartbroken from the field, their players deserve to be told one thing: They gave the country the greatest FA Cup Final in recent memory. Perhaps one of the greatest of all time… For West Ham try valiant, gallant, daring. Not words that are usually associated with failure. If failure this was."

The *Evening Standard* runs with, "Silver lining in great show of pride… West Ham fans have a lot to look forward to despite the agony of defeat."

The *Sun's* banner above all its multi-page coverage reads "BEST FINAL EVER," while Steven Howard writes of a "Claret and blue rhapsody." It has pictures of Anton Ferdinand and Yossi Benayoun fighting back tears, while ex-Hammer Tony Gale has the best line: "They say you never remember the losers at the FA Cup Final — well, this year we will."

Alan Pardew refuses to criticize Scaloni, even when asked by reporters if the full-back has cost West Ham the final, and tells the media: "I've told the players in the dressing room that they have taken part in one of the greatest Cup Finals. They can take that with them, as well as pride in their performance... if I build well and recruit well, we have the base of a very good team."

This being West Ham, it would never prove to be that simple. It should have been the basis of a fine side. But in December 2006 the new Icelandic owners of the club sacked Pardew. Dean Ashton broke his ankle training with England, missed a season and eventually had to retire. Nigel Reo-Coker became dissatisfied after a move to Arsenal fell through and eventually joined Aston Villa. Yossi Benayoun went to Liverpool, Harewood stopped scoring and several players succumbed to the Baby Bentley culture.

While Liverpool fans could forever taunt the Irons' supporters with chants of, "Two-nil and you f**ked it up!"

But on that May day West Ham were the better side and should have won the FA Cup. As Pardew said: "Nothing can take away the pride and respect I have for my players after the way they represented West Ham United."

And in one way it was a victory. In the Premier League era that classic six-goal final restored the glory to the so-often devalued FA Cup.

10. NOTHING BEATS BEING BACK

2012 CHAMPIONSHIP PLAY-OFF FINAL

WEST HAM UNITED 2 BLACKPOOL 1

Wembley Stadium, Saturday May 19 2012. Kick-off 3pm.

WEST HAM: Robert Green, Guy Demel (Faubert 57), James Tomkins, Winston Reid, Matt Taylor, Gary O'Neil (McCartney 53), Kevin Nolan, Mark Noble, Jack Collison, Ricardo Vaz Te, Carlton Cole.
Substitutes: Stephen Henderson, Julien Faubert, George McCartney, Henri Lansbury, Nicky Maynard.

IF THE KITS ARE UNITED: Claret and blue shirts with 'SBOBET' sponsorship logo, white shirts, white socks with claret and blue band, multicoloured boots. Claret 'Nothing beats being back' t-shirts worn for presentation of trophy.

FACIAL HAIR: Ricardo Vaz Te has a Kid Creole-style pencil-moustache. Stubble-come-beard sported by substitute Julien Faubert.

BLOW DRY FACTOR: Ricardo Vaz Te has a chunky Mohican, Mark Noble a 1950s proper footballer side-parting, Robert Green a rockabilly wedge top over a short back and sides.

FLYING SO HIGH: WEST HAM'S CUP FINALS

FAN FACTOR: Flags, claret and blue fuzzy wigs, beach balls, balloons, bubbles, claret and blue scarves, various replica shirts, 'Sex and drugs and Carlton Cole' banner, West Ham scarf on statue of Bobby Moore.

ATTENDANCE: 78,523.

PRICE OF PROGRAMME: £6

It's been 31 years… and now there's claret and blue again on Wembley Way. West Ham are playing at Wembley for the first time since the League Cup Final of 1981 and the FA Cup victory of 1980. The three finals the club reached in the new millennium, the Championship Play-Off finals in 2004 and 2005 and the FA Cup Final of 2006, have all been played at the Millennium Stadium.

Technically it's not a cup-final, of course, but it is in all but name. The Play-Off final is billed as the most expensive game in football. The winner can expect an increase in revenue of £40 million plus the following season.

In 2012 David Cameron is Prime Minster of austerity Britain, Roy Hodgson is the new England gaffer, Matt Smith is the Doctor, the *News of the World* is no more, there's an inquiry into phone hacking, banks aren't what we thought they were and the European single currency is unravelling. But none of that matters anymore because WHU are at Wem-ber-ley.

Sam Allardyce's men have been unlucky to miss out on automatic promotion, finishing third with 86 points. In the previous season Norwich had been promoted as runners-up with 84 points. Too many home draws have cost the side, though Sam Allardyce had transformed the club's away record and signed virtually a new team of players.

West Ham record a stunning 13 away victories setting a new club record. The Play-Off semi-final has seen a 5-0 aggregate defeat of Cardiff City. Jack Collison's double wins the game at Cardiff and goals from Nolan, Vaz Te and Maynard seal a 3-0 home win to take the club to Wembley.

These days are special. It's hard not to think of Billy Bonds lifting the cup twice, Trevor Brooking's header, Alan Taylor's goals, the White Horse final and Bobby Moore running round the stadium with a giant hammer and *Bubbles* wafting around Wembley as Moore receives the Cup Winners Cup in 1965.

I'm at the game with my two daughters and I'm proud of my paternal role in helping them to become part of West Ham's Wembley lineage.

Wembley Way is packed with claret and blue and orange. Stalls sell £6 programmes, split club souvenir scarves, and £10 flags, though you do get a free bubbles jar with every purchase. Hammers fans throng around the giant Bobby Moore Statue on the concourse. In the Club Wembley section of the stadium you can buy a £6 Lincolnshire sausage, and a £4 pre-match bottle of Carlsberg.

The programme has no adverts for Double Diamond or Player's No 6. Instead it's Kia Sportage cars, Woodycouture bulldogs, Powerade sports drinks, Samsung Galaxy smartphones, Shore Capital corporate finance, the Blizzard, a digital quarterly football publication, and proving how the gender divide at matches has changed, Beko washing machines, an advert aimed at 'mums united.' There are no Rizla adverts on the pitchside hoardings either, but rolling electronic npower and Carling slogans.

The West Ham half of the stadium is heaving and there's a beach ball bouncing around. Cross of St George flags are draped over balconies with things like "Billericay Irons" written on them. A huge claret and blue flag with Bobby Moore's face on it is passed over the heads of the fans. A banner at the front reads, "Sex and drugs and Carlton Cole."

The Blackpool end is a colourful wall of orange but has 12,000 empty seats in the upper tiers. Kevin Nolan's family alone could have taken that many seats. There's no marching band in 2012, just great big npower balloons, TV screens showing the players in the tunnel and the PA playing *Bubbles* for the West Ham fans.

At 3pm the game begins with West Ham kicking towards the Blackpool fans. Any confidence among the Irons contingent soon evaporates in the first 15 minutes. In the third minute Dobbie brushes past Matt Taylor to force a good low save from Rob Green at his near post. In response Vaz Te dribbles into the Blackpool box, but from close to the byline blazes wildly across goal.

Matt Phillips drifts through the centre of the static Hammers defence for a one-on-one chance, only to shoot tamely at Green. Then Demel hesitates and loses the ball in calamitous fashion to let in Matt Phillips who cuts in from the left and curls a shot just wide of the post.

West Ham are looking nervous; Demel doesn't appear to be fully fit, Reid is looking overawed, Collison takes a long time to get into the game, and the mobile Ince and Matt Phillips have the beating of the Hammers' full-backs.

But slowly West Ham settle. Vaz Te shoots into the side netting after a good lay-off by Cole, when he should probably score. West Ham force four successive corners. It looks like the Irons have got over their wobble on 35 minutes. Matt Taylor plays in a perfect cross from the left and Carlton Cole gets behind Evatt to control brilliantly and fire into the roof of the net.

Carlton runs to the fans at the side of the stadium, as Matt Taylor leaps on his back. "Come on you Irons!" and *I'm Forever Blowing Bubbles* are the soundtrack as Blackpool kick-off.

A few minutes later Vaz Te pokes a good chance wide after an excellent pass by O'Neil. That would have settled the game.

Half-time seems to last only ten minutes and most of the crowd are still in the bar as Blackpool make a lively start. Reid stops one attack with a fine tackle.

Then, three minutes into the second half, Carlton Cole loses the ball on the half-way line and ironically the Hammers are undone by a long ball from Phillips. Thomas Ince gets beyond Matt Taylor and the covering Reid and connects decisively to poke the ball past Green.

A goal scored by the son of ex-Hammer Paul Ince. The WHU fans have horrible visions of those "Ince Perfect" headlines tomorrow. Undone by a side who can't sell out their end.

"You're not singing anymore!" chants the wall of orange (with several bricks missing).

Blackpool have the better of the second half. At least West Ham improve a bit defensively when McCartney comes on for O'Neil and Taylor moves into midfield, and Faubert replaces Demel. West Ham's whole season rests on French novelist Julien 'Gustave' Faubert.... The Gallic right-back finds Carlton Cole, who has a turn and shot excellently saved by Gilks, but it's a rare foray.

Taylor has to clear off the line from Baptiste and then Dobbie goes all house elf from *Harry Potter*, scuffing wide a superb chance that Kevin Phillips would surely have buried. Noble has to clear off the line from a corner. Collison replies with a shot over the bar. Dobbie forces Green to save low down and then fires a free kick straight at the keeper. It seems like the game's only just into the second half, but there's 80 minutes on the scoreboard.

"We are Bobby Moore's claret and blue army!" chant the Hammers fans, trying to rally the side. And then "My name is Ludek Miklosko I come from near Moscow! I play in goal for West Ham!"

Time's passing as quickly as it did in the horrible Play-Off final loss to Palace in 2004. Most

West Ham fans are picturing a late Blackpool winner and Ian Holloway jigging around the pitch having "got the bird in the taxi" to use his gentleman's metaphor.

The Irons need Nolan to suddenly produce one of those goals he scores after seemingly drifting out of the game. Sure enough, McCartney puts in a great cross and Kevin Nolan hits the bar with a superb full volley, just tipped on to the bar by Gilks. It could be West Ham's last chance to win it. Surely not extra time and penalties...

There's nearly 87 minutes gone as the ball comes to Nolan on the left. He cuts inside and crosses low into the box. Carlton Cole controls and pulls the ball past a defender and just as the keeper tries to smother it, he pokes the ball out of his hands and back to Vaz Te who is surely going to hit the bar or hoof it into the stand, but now it's in the roof of the net. GOAAAAAL!

The West Ham end is exploding with joy and relief and people are hugging each other and waving flags and wondering if this is West Ham's Man City-style 'Aguero moment'. Ricardo whips off his shirt and struts in front of the West Ham fans. It's worth the yellow card he receives. "We are going up! I said we are going up!" chant three tiers of reverberating fans.

It's apt the goal has been made by Carlton Cole. In this game he's been immense. Maybe it's due to the two-week break before the final, but finally he looks fully fit. Cole has had plenty of abuse on online forums for not scoring enough compared to Southampton's Ricky Lambert. But today he's netted a great goal, set up a clear opportunity for Vaz Te to shoot wide, forced a great save from Gilks, made the second goal and led the line with a performance of real character.

That goal is also the culmination of an amazing season for Ricardo Vaz Te. Signed for just £500,000, he's scored 24 goals in a season, 12 goals for the Hammers and 12 for Barnsley. All this after it looked as if he was drifting out of the game having failed to establish himself at Bolton and ended up playing the previous season for Greek side Panionis and Hibernian in Scotland.

Two minutes left. Big Sam chews his thousandth piece of gum. In the stands Geoff Hurst looks nervous, 47 years to the day after he played in the West Ham side that won the Cup Winners' Cup at Wembley. "Let's go f**king mental! La la la la!" sing the West Ham fans.

There's four minutes of injury time to endure and the ball fizzes agonisingly across the West Ham box. Cole gets hold of it up front and the players manage to keep it in the corner and then survive a dubious penalty appeal as Dicko tumbles after a challenge from Reid. The ball is kicked upfield by Robert Green and then the whistle goes and it's over! Ricardo Vaz Te runs to the fans gyrating his arms, doing a cool victory shuffle.

"West Ham United are Promoted to the Premier League!" announces the PA. "Never in (much) doubt," I suggest.

"You know, I think I might renew my season ticket," suggests my fellow season-ticket holder Nigel.

Kevin Nolan walks up about ten-thousand steps to collect the trophy wearing a claret and blue scarf and with a flag tied round his neck as if it were a cape. The whole team are now wearing 'Nothing Beats Being Back' t-shirts and have medals round their necks. Nolan's followed by Mark Noble and Robert Green, two of the key performers of the season.

Karren Brady is hugging David Gold and Big Sam. David Sullivan appears to be wiping away a tear, or is he just thinking of all those contracts that revert to Premier League wages?

Nolan lifts the trophy with a passionate yell of triumph as *Paradise* by Coldplay plays over the PA. "Para... para... paradise! Whoa whoa!" Fireworks explode on the pitch. My daughters are seeing West Ham win a trophy and the players get a medal each at Wembley. This only happens once every 31 years. Nell blows bubbles, Lola waves her chequered claret and blue flag.

"Their first visit to the new Wembley has yielded their first win at the new Wembley. Mission accomplished!" is the commentary on Sky TV as Kevin lifts the trophy. "An astonishing end to an at times turbulent season."

Sam Allardyce has both hands on the trophy. There's even a *Paradise*-style chant of "Allar... Allar... Allar... Allardyce" from some West Ham fans. And Big Sam is actually smiling. His tenure has been controversial at the Academy of Football, but the man has given the club its first Wembley win in 31 years.

Allardyce so often resembles some curmudgeonly character from a Samuel Beckett play standing glum-faced on the touchline, but here he is looking like he is genuinely enjoying being the manager of West Ham United and starting to realise the full potential of the club.

The lads run on to the pitch and pose for a team shot with the trophy. Mark Noble has a jester's hat on and is preparing to take his winners medal to Dubai for his stag party. Vaz Te dances, Carlton Cole dons a claret and blue wig as he's interviewed by ITV. Kevin Nolan says it's one of the best days of his life.

Sam Allardyce embraces James Tomkins in a paternal manner and says, in a manner strangely reminiscent of Windsor Davies in *It Ain't Half Hot Mum*. "Never such a handsome centre half have I met or coached, but what a player!" Fine pair of shoulders there son, show 'em off.

The PA plays *Hi Ho Silver Lining*, *Rockin' All Over The World* and *We Are The Champions* and my kids are singing along to *Twist and Shout* and then another chorus of *Bubbles*.

"Will we be able to buy Scott Parker back now?" asks my 11-year-old daughter Nell, and I tell her he might well want to move to a club with a more realistic chance of making the Champions League than Spurs. "That's if he could get into our side!"

"He scores when he wants! He scores when he wants! Ricardo Vaz Te... he scores when he wants!" sing the joyous claret and blue hordes. Outside Wembley someone has risked serious injury and draped a Hammers scarf around the lofty statue of Bobby Moore. The fans sing: "We are Premier League; I said we are Premier League!"

Our party eventually finds a dodgy pub in Wembley with a moth-infested carpet in the back-room, but we don't care, it's full of joyous Hammers and my pals Fraser and CQ are smoking celebratory cigars.

After that we head home via Marylebone station, where "Ricardo Vaz Te, he scores when he wants!" is being sung on the concourse. Then it's champagne with my wife Nicola in the kitchen and *Bubbles* on the CD player.

After the game Carlton Cole tweets that he's played with an injury for the last eight weeks. He tells reporters: "I've kept my mouth shut for quite a while, but I did take a big pay-cut to stay in the Championship – half my wages went at a stroke, but I wanted to help the club get back to where it belongs."

His wages have reportedly fallen to around 14k a week, which, while not exactly leaving him short of the price of a full breakfast in Ken's Cafe, does show his commitment when he could have moved to Stoke or Turkey for big money. Cole has a real feeling for the club, to judge by his tweet: "West Ham have shown me a home. I'm happy here as long as they want me." He deserves his "Sex and Drugs and Carlton Cole" banner.

There's some minor Champions League Final being played in Munich that evening, between Bayern Munich and Chelsea. The Blues' win on penalties takes up much of the press coverage in the following days, with the much bigger game at Wembley downplayed.

But The *Guardian* devotes two pages to the Play-Off final, with a headline referring to the need for more finance: "Allardyce gets his way and prize but the future hangs on Gold digging." This is accompanied by a large double-page spread picture of Vaz Te rippling the Blackpool net.

The *Daily Mirror* manages to maintain its tradition for including every cockney cliché going in its match report, including "bubble blowers, pearly kings and *Knees Up Mother Brown* tendency", "45,000 jellied eel connoisseurs" and Carlton Cole's loyalty earning him a place among "East End legends like Bobby Moore, Geoff Hurst, Martin Peters, Trevor Brooking and Dot Cotton."

It might only be a Play-Off final for some. But this game in 2012 joins the West Ham United-significant dates of 1964, 1965, 1975, 1980 and 2006.

It's the fifth Wembley victory for West Ham and with so much money resting on promotion to the Premier League and the club in massive debt; it's possibly the most vital. Automatic promotion would have been far too simple and much less romantic. For football is surely all about dreams and moments of glory punctuating the more familiar tales of underachievement.

Hopefully there will be more finals to come for West Ham, and somewhat more regularly, with all the heroics of Bobby Moore, Ronnie Boyce, Alan Sealey, Alan Taylor, Trevor Brooking, Dean Ashton and Ricardo Vaz Te repeated by stars yet to emerge. And remember, West Ham haven't lost a final at Wembley since 1923… Come on you Irons!

THE OTHER CUP FINALS

West Ham have reached several other Cup Finals, apart from the great moments included in this book. *Flying So High* was originally published as an e-book, so for reasons of length not all of these have been included.

The Hammers also reached the League Cup Final in 1966, losing to West Bromwich Albion 5-2 on aggregate, the year before the final was moved to Wembley.

West Ham won the Inter-Toto Cup Final against Metz in August 1999, winning 3-1 away after losing the fist leg 1-0 at Upton Park. Though the tournament was derided by some, it was still a notable victory as it secured UEFA Cup football.

West Ham lost 1 0 to Crystal Palace in the 2004 Championship Play-Off Final at Cardiff's Millennium Stadium.

West Ham also won the 1940 Football League War Cup Final at Wembley. The kick off was at 6.30 pm and the match was watched by 42,300 despite the fear of bombing by the Luftwaffe. The Irons beat Blackburn Rovers 1-0 through a goal from Sam Small.

Acknowledgements

Thanks to everyone at Endeavour who has helped with the production of the electronic version of this book, and of course my fellow West Ham fans for shared endurance, including Nigel Morris, Fraser Massey, Matt George, Lisa Pritchard, Michael McManus, Denis Campbell, Gavin Hadland and Joe Norris, plus numerous other Irons, the Newham Bookshop and all at Ken's Café.

My research has been helped by many books, including *West Ham United: The Elite Era* by John Helliar, *West Ham United* by Charles Korr, *The Lads of '23* by Brian Belton, *Hammers in Focus* by Steve Bacon, *Sincerely Yours* by Ron Greenwood, *Just Like My Dreams* by John Lyall, *1966 and All That* by Geoff Hurst, *Bobby Moore* by Jeff Powell, *Bonzo* by Billy Bonds, *Trevor Brooking* by Trevor Brooking, cuttings from the *East Ham Echo* and the DVDs of all the various finals.

And of course I'd like to thank my wife Nicola and daughters Lola and Nell, who might one day even see a cup or two or more for West Ham and the claret and blue.

Pete May, London, 2012

ALSO BY PETE MAY

Man About Tarn
Goodbye to Boleyn
Whovian Dad
The Joy of Essex
There's A Hippo In My Cistern
Hammers In The Heart
Ageing Body Confused Mind
Rent Boy
West Ham: Irons In The Soul
Sunday Muddy Sunday
The Lad Done Bad
Football and its Followers
World Cup Expert: Players
World Cup Expert: Teams

Pete May blogs on West Ham at
hammersintheheart.blogspot.co.uk

Printed in Great Britain
by Amazon

44373184R00081